The People's History

Cop On The Tyne

by

Arthur McKenzie

My children, Andrew and Kirsty, lend a hand but it's no good we can't get it up. A totally natural photograph – no (h)airbrushing whatsoever.

Previous page: PC 430 – on point duty Pilgrim Street Foot, July 1964 – where I was sent to supervise the destruction of a wonderful group of buildings including the Arcade – to be replaced by soulless monstrosities.

Copyright © Arthur McKenzie 2001

First published in 2001 by

The People's History Ltd
Suite 1, Byron House
Seaham Grange Business Park
Seaham, Co. Durham
SR7 0PY

ISBN 1 902527 74 7

Contents

Foreword

I am sure that in all jobs people look back to a golden age. The time when real characters did the work, bureaucracy was minimal and results were achieved which the present generation would never even aspire to

One of the real characters from a golden age of policing is Arthur McKenzie. In a career spanning the full and varying roles from patrol officer in Newcastle to senior detecting in the Regional Crime Squad and the International Commission Against Corruption in Hong Kong, Arthur demonstrated outstanding levels of policing ability and tenacity. When police officers from my generation meet, the conversation will invariably at some stage return to our Golden Age. Sometimes, as in the Lords of the Rings the 'tale will grow in the telling'. Arthur McKenzie is a regular subject for the discussion in these police folk tales. With Arthur, however, the true story is often more astonishing and entertaining than the collective memory.

I worked with Arthur over many years. I was a player in some of the adventures. When I was a young detective I viewed Arthur with a mixture of awe and admiration. He was possessed of enormous physical strength and an active, enquiring mind. He combined these two attributes in devastating combination against the criminal. In retrospect I think that Arthur was able to produce a synergy from his basic skills. He was able to refine technique.

This technique, clearly counted in his policing career but perhaps that same combination of strength, intellect and technique were most clearly seen in his achievements as an international athlete, and in his subsequent career as a writer.

Arthur has a tale to tell. I want to read it.

Alan Oliver, QPM
Former Assistant Chief Constable, Northumbria Police

Introduction – Who is Arthur McKenzie?

As a young man in the mid 1950s Arthur left his home town of North Shields to accidentally join Newcastle City Police. This 'tip toe in a tunic' covers those first thirteen years of his life as a constable in times of change, excitement and freedom.

It was different society then, different rules, different attitudes, and he makes no excuse for the anecdotes and opinions for that is what he was – a hairy arsed polis. No quarter given or taken, he was proud to be a member of Newcastle City Police. The streets were patrolled firmly, but fairly and it was safe to go into the town without fear of being robbed or assaulted. Life was much simpler, the 'Bobby on the Beat' a clear figure of authority who, in the main, commanded the respect of the public and in return endeavoured to give good service.

Come the 1970s that all changed when a succession of boundary amalgamations and progressive ideas began to undermine the public perception and trust in the police service. Introduction of panda cars, while making officers more mobile, created a 'fire brigade' system separating police from the public, then the highly divisive miners' strike created a para-military styled service further eroding public's confidence. Of course those weren't the only causes, crime patterns, mobility of criminals, computers and access to and dissemination of information meant the job had to keep pace with society. So change was inevitable, but whether it was for the better is the big question.

Cop On The Tyne is a personal insight of what it was like to be a policeman in what many regard as the golden years. In the same uncompromising style as his policing he describes the highs, lows, personalities and prejudices. It wasn't all milk and honey, he made enemies, many on his own side of the fence, but it didn't prevent him enjoying every minute of his incredible service. Throughout he attempts to embrace his subject matter with honesty and integrity, but most of all it is his humour and zest for the job which shines through as he shares with us a peep into a period of time many people wish could return.

In boxing and in life you always want the very best people in your corner and I am proud Arthur McKenziehas always been in mine. A man who strives to be the best in everything he does and achieved it in his work as a policeman, athlete and now as a writer. I am only glad he never decided to box because I'm sure he would of beat me to be the first North East World Champion.

Glenn McCrory

A study of my mother as a young woman on Warkworth beach by my father. He had a consuming passion for photography and he left a legacy of hundreds of prints of local scenes and family portraits from the 1920s. A photograph captures a second of life and his eye for mood and light was remarkable. Many of the photographs in this book were taken by him and I will forever be in his debt for his vision.

My mother and I never really saw eye to eye ... it was an adolescent thing. She never knew what I was or what I became, but I know she was proud because her last words to the nurse in the hospital, before she died, were: 'My son's on the Force.'

This book is in celebration of her and the rest of my family who have somehow retained their sanity and sense of humour while I rode a ridiculous rollercoaster.

Arthur McKenzie
2001

FROM WAR BABY TO WOR BABY

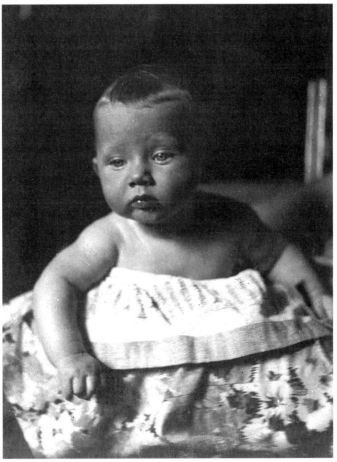

They say a new born baby smells of freshly baked bread, who would have thought this one would have turned into a grim faced detective – taken in Guyzance in 1939.

I close my eyes and see it clearly, October 1958, same old routine, half past seven in the morning, bleary eyed, I'm standing on Preston Road at the foot of Camp Terrace, North Shields, in a police cadet's uniform, waiting for the 'Red Rattler' to take me to Newcastle. For over three years I'd persevered that eight miles to the Haymarket and the bones of my arse knew every pothole and ridge intimately. Each day I would use the journey to reflect on how I'd actually arrived at that time and place in my life, because sure as God made little apples I'd certainly never set out to be a polis. The whole thing was a complete mystery to me.

A war baby, I was born Arthur Thomas McKenzie on the 14th April 1939 in a classic suburban semi, 56 Sunlea Avenue, Cullercoats. Arthur taken from my father, and Thomas after grandfather on my mother's side. Memories of air raid warnings, being snatched from my cot to spend endless nights in a damp air raid shelter are as if yesterday. I also remember being petrified as clusters of guns on The Broadway banged away over the sea, but my lasting image is of the barrage balloon which lay like a tethered grey whale on Tynemouth golf course. For many years a lump of glistening shrapnel, which hit our roof, was proudly displayed in the china cabinet.

My father was a solicitor's clerk with Reed, Ryder and Meikle in North Shields where he remained from the age of 12 until the day he died at 77. My mother, a country girl from Guyzance, a tiny row of cottages near Warkworth, was an innocent, gentle soul, who never really got to grips with the twentieth century. She knew little of the outside world and actually believed what people told her, something I found very difficult to comprehend. Brother Walter was a year and ten months younger than me and at four and five respectively we both ran

View of North Shields in the 1920s – The haze from the Guano Fish Works is clearly visible. An excellent study by my father.

away from home and attempted to launch a rowing boat in Cullercoats Bay to explore lands across the sea, but he filled his pants, bringing that adventure to a smelly, sticky end. Not long after that he broke my leg with a sideboard drawer and, ever since, he and I have kept each other at a respectful, but brotherly distance. My childhood was relatively happy, but I never could get to grips with early school, my main concern being I always seemed to fail when the rides on the rocking horse in the corner of the hall were allocated.

When the war ended we moved to 19 Sandringham Gardens in North Shields. A four bedroom terrace, it offered more space for my grandparents on my mother's side. Grandma had had a stroke, and it was felt she would be better cared for in that family environment. This put immense pressure on my parents, especially my mother, who sacrificed her life to look after them. Shields was, and still is, a rough, tough town on the coastline of Northumberland, with a history steeped in fish guts. The folk are solid, friendly and dependable, but even as a young kid I thought it was in a time warp. Okay, there were the pits,

My mother and father's wedding day on 21st August 1927. The photograph was taken at the family's cottage in Guyzance. Standing: Uncle Tommy Tully, dad, mam and Granda Tully. Seated: Grandma Elizabeth McKenzie and Grandma Isabella Tully.

Fishing boats bobbing at North Shields Fish Quay in the 1920s when it had a thriving industry – again taken by my father. North Shields Fish Quay was always a source of mystery and adventure. The smells, noise and sheer vibrancy made it a compulsive and dangerous playground.

trawlers, and building work, but nothing to stimulate a brave new world, so from very early on I made a conscious decision to break away from it at the first opportunity.

The neighbours to both sides of us were, shall we say a little different. One, a retired local barber, who looked like Winston Churchill, would cut our hair with a basin and a pair of clippers. To the other side was a brother and sister. She was an instructress at Rigby's school of dancing, but he was slightly odd and continually pestered us for scraps of bread and pieces of fat as if such things were just lying around the house. He would then take these oddments of food to the Black Midden rocks and whistle. Believe it or not rats would appear and he would feed them by hand and we were always concerned in case he decided to bring any lame ones home for recuperation.

My early schooling was extremely spasmodic because I was a sickly child. At seven I caught pleurisy and nearly died, so education didn't as much pass me by, it just didn't interfere with my life. In Shields I attended King Edward Junior School on Preston Avenue where I was constantly bullied and spent most of my time hiding from the gangs.

I find it difficult to actually remember much about it except for pain, playing milk tops and 'muggles' against a wall. My 'aunt' Maggie once took me from the infants to visit a friend nearby and I was terrified of the parrot in the dining room. Failing the eleven plus I then went to Jubilee School at the corner of Albion and Preston Roads opposite Ye Olde 100 pub. An old workhouse come hospital and soup kitchen it had been converted into a school. It consisted of a cold hall and all classrooms had large fireplaces where coal fires constantly burned to prevent us getting hypothermia. Again the bulk of my time was spent day dreaming and watching pigeons on the Catholic Church window sill opposite. Highlight of the day would be playtime when we'd swap wonderful crisp-smelling American comics (Batman, Superman and Spiderman) which were just coming onto the market.

Growing up after the war everything seemed exciting and because my parents' time was fully taken up with looking after Grandma and Granda Tulley, who was now going senile, I was left to run free. Everything was exciting, climbing trees in Preston Park, riding the horses there bare back and birds nesting. Exploring the Gut on the fish quay, taking the ferry to South Shields and climbing over the arches to the bridge were regular past times. If my mother had found out she would have collapsed with anxiety. I once got captured riding two on a

Dad when he was in Newcastle's Special Constabulary (Mounted Section). The photograph was taken at a riding school in Benton in 1936.

Mam, all dressed up and ready for church. It is great to be able to remember my mother looking so happy and serene – because her life was going to bring her much heartache and stress.

bike on the footpath by a copper. You'd think I was an acid bath killer. I was wheeled in front of the Chief Constable with my mate to be cautioned and made to promise never to be taken into the police station again. Little did I know what life had in store.

I vaguely remember passing the 'over age examination' and gained a scholarship to Tynemouth High School. Another total mystery, but sheer joy to my parents. Again it was more day dreaming, with the only interests woodwork, rugby and athletics, the latter turning out to be a complete revelation. It was in the last year of school and this lunch time in particular I was on the field looking for trouble, watching a lad throwing the discus. Suddenly the implement bounced and rolled towards my feet. Never having touched one in my life I picked it up, shouted at the kid who'd thrown it, chased him and swung the discus in his direction, fully expecting it to land short. Much to my surprise it flew over his head and then I heard the games master Mr Banks shouting and running after me. Fully expecting a sand-shoe (his favourite instrument) across my backside I braced, but the blow never came. He was puffing and panting.

'Don't you realise what you've done McKenzie?'

'I didn't want to hit him sir.'

'No you idiot! You've just broken the county record!' And from that moment I became a fanatic on discus throwing and that ridiculous incident eventually changed the course of my life.

After pleurisy I had a terrible spell of illness and this actually drove me towards becoming locked into fitness. I subscribed to a Charles Atlas Course and followed its dynamic tension techniques rigorously and gradually built myself up. It most certainly prevented anyone else kicking sand in my face. Daily I would do chin ups from the stair head every time I came down and this gave me confidence. An older pal of mine made me up a set of dumb bells at the shipyard and every night before going to bed I would crash them around in my bedroom, playing havoc with the ceiling below.

Academia had long passed by, and the time I should have spent honing my mind to become a brain surgeon or industrial chemist was basically spent spitting on other kids at school or putting dead mice behind radiators. Spitting? I nearly got expelled for that. The headmaster publicly vilified me at assembly but I didn't really care because it gave me status.

'This gross act was performed by a disgusting, filthy boy.'

So, the only qualifications I had as I hurried from the school gates on that last day were: I could make an elliptical mat and had been awarded athletics colours having been county champion at the discus. Against all the odds I also gained one GSE in English Language, but only God's agents know how that was achieved, because I didn't do a scrap of work.

By then I'd become a pretend teddy boy, chains on my shoes, semi crew and boot lace tie. Buying the real clobber at an outfitters such as City Stylish, Newcastle was way beyond my means and that meant sewing in my own trousers to sixteen inches and cutting pieces of

My class at King Edward School in 1948. I am standing in the second back row next to the teacher on the right.

National Association of Boys Clubs, 1955 – being presented with my International Rugby colours at Smith's Park North Shields. Harry Martin (centre) saved me from going onto the other side of the tracks with his encouragement and support.

chains for my shoes. The hair cut was achieved by running a comb with a razor blade attached, Brylcream as stiff as starch; and the Tony Curtis look with a D.A. (duck's arse) at the back was incredible. Posing at the fish shop in Queen Alexandra Road or walking along the sea front from Cullercoats to the Whitley Bay amusements were highlights of the week. Whitley Bay had all the bright lights and excitement and we would spend the little money we had feeding Wurlitzer juke boxes playing Bill Haley's *Rock Around the Clock* and other decadent devil music while lounging at the slot machines. Girls were there, but only just. We were more interested in how we looked, and fighting. Without a job or prospects I didn't have a clue where the adventure was going to take me. Again I didn't care and a good pal of mine tried to persuade me to go on the whalers with him, when another mate suggested we went to Newcastle to join the police cadets. I mean, where had he got that notion from? A copper was the last thing anybody wanted to be, but for moral support I tagged along for the giggle.

The cop shop at the corner of Pilgrim Street and Market Street looked more like an Art Nouveau hotel. Formidable, the revolving doors propelled us into a new world smelling of honeysuckle floor polish. There was one of them dinger bells on a desk so I banged it a

My James Dean period – 1954 taken at my mate's house in West Percy Road, Ridges Estate, North Shields. I remember we set up the shot like professionals – a light bulb masked with cardboard and the look angled just right at a mark on the ceiling. What a couple of right painful pillocks we must have been.

Brother Walter – younger, cleverer, a far better athlete and poser than me – but we always kept a healthy relationship after he broke my leg with a drawer.

couple of times much to the annoyance of a large man who appeared from behind a glass partition and demanded, 'What the hell do you think you are doing?'

I explained, 'He wants to join you lot.' This large man turned out to be storeman George Bone, who also doubled as recruiting officer. He gave my mate a sniffy once over.

'You're not big enough son.'

'I'm five eleven,' says my mate holding himself up to his full height.

'Na, take it from me son. I'm measuring people every day and y'not. You're five seven top whack. Try the fire brigade. They're looking for lads like you.'

And that was it! Dismissed! Then he raked a gimlet eye over me. 'You're a big lad.'

'Aye, I'm from Shields.'

'So, how about it?'

'Me? A polis? Nee way. What? I'd never be able to hold me head up again.' Undeterred, he pressed an application form into my hand. Resistance was impossible.

'Hey, it's him what wants to join man … he's keen. That's what you want isn't it, keen people? I've got plans, there's plenty of graft man. Buildings, forestry. My mate wants me to go on the whalers. The *Kista Dan* … you heard of it?'

'Aye it's a Norwegian ship but if you want to fight sailors properly get y'sel two referees,' he smiled, his teeth dropped then clacked back into place.

'Two referees? Is it a football match like?' His look rendered me down like bacon in a frying pan.

'What's the matter, frightened of a man's job son?'

'Frightened? I could do it standing on me head.' More of George later, but he'd put me right in the frame. My mate? Years later he became my best man, but after I married disappeared and I never saw him again.

So, I had to run the gauntlet when mam found the dreaded forms in my pocket. We were having big rows now, I was a handful, and once kicked the banisters out and threw an electric fire through the kitchen window. I'm not proud of behaviour which must have terrified her and my future looked bleak. She was going through a rough time looking after her parents, and seeing me galloping headlong down the track to disgrace must have been frightening. Her brother, my uncle Tommy was a policeman in Northumberland, but we had little to do with him. It did, however, motivate her to convince me that it was a steady job with, as they say, 'prospects'.

To keep the peace I reluctantly filled out the forms and got a respected bloke who ran a Bible class at dad's Memorial Methodist Church on Albion Road to act as one of the referees. I can remember thinking it was bad enough applying for the police without bringing church into it. In my naiveté I didn't reckon on a cat in hell's chance, but after a couple of weeks was summoned to the Central Police Station for a written examination.

Come the fateful day I found myself sitting in a large class-type room in the upper reaches of the police station along with another twenty hopefuls. A sergeant welcomed us to the exam and told us we must not cheat. The atmosphere was very much one of quiet discipline so there was very little chat between us as George Bone rolled in and laid out the exam papers and sharpened pens for the use of, his teeth clacking constantly. I couldn't believe the questions ... 'Where are the Ural Mountains?' ... 'What is the Sargasso Sea famous for?' ... Then some simple arithmetic and a piece of précis. None of it had anything to do with being a hairy arsed polis, but I got this feeling when I walked through that classroom door my height had it all cut and dried. George Bone marked the papers and gave me a most alarming wink.

The interview was a doddle, some inspector in the training department along with the sergeant. I forget who they were now, but their probing interview concentrated on the fact that I loved sport and they seemed to be impressed by the Bible class write up. It was all very depressing knowing I had been accepted, then this was compounded by the words, 'Okay son, we'll have you for a medical.' What gripped me was, despite my resistance, somehow I'd been pressurised and sucked into it all. I looked round the police station as I headed for the revolving doors and thought, 'No, this is definitely not for me ... I'm a free spirit.'

Hell broke out at home when I told my parents I wasn't going through with it – a real shouting match which came to the crunchers when dad told me in no uncertain manner if I didn't attend the medical I'd have to find alternative lodgings. Dad, a strict Methodist who only ever drank water, never lost his temper so I knew when he delivered the ultimatum he meant it.

At the time there was terrific tension in the house and being adolescent I thought it was down to me, but on reflection it all came through my grandad. Poor old bugger, I can still see him vivid, smoking tea leaves, because 'baccy' was expensive. He'd dry them in little piles on the backyard step. Grandad was a big solid man of few words from Warkworth. A stone mason by trade he'd done much of the restoration work on the Castle and then took over the tenancy of the Black Bull in the village. I still have strong memories of being wheeled with my brother in a barrow from his allotment in Guyzance during the war. The small cottage in which he and grandma lived was lit by oil lamps and we would sit in front of the open range toasting bread on the end of a long fork. He was always strong and in control, but when he came to live in Shields spent most of his time in his room. Whenever I took a cup of tea or something to him this lonely figure would just stare at me with his light blue watery eyes.

His main feature was a huge nose which had a large growth on the end, like a semi deflated balloon. When he pushed it with his hanky the mass would move up over his face and hide an eye. Mam bought him a special cup with a moulded section indented so his nose would fit in and be prevented from being burned by the hot tea. I found out later this was a form of gout. He virtually lived in his room and did his pools, probably thought people would stare at him. And they did, for any deformity has its own form of magnetism.

We had many dramatic moments in his later stages of senility because he would shout and scream in the middle of the night, thrashing about, but the worst situation arose when he locked himself in the bathroom and attempted to drown himself in the bath. He put a broom across the door so we couldn't get in and it was one hell of a job breaking it down to force him out. I ended up pulling a few more out of baths in my time. This stressful background, me struggling with adolescence and my grandad passing me on the way back to his second childhood made life difficult for all of us. Mam and dad loved me, but I can't remember any cuddling or anything like that, so communication between us was always strained. It wasn't until many years later that I found out she was agoraphobic and terrified of the world ... she thought it was a terrible place!

So suddenly my nightmare became a reality and I found myself standing in this half baked doctor's surgery in deepest Walker in the East End of Newcastle. Stevo's place – Doctor Stevenson. Flicking through the curly cornered Punch magazines I wondered if I'd fallen asleep and woken up in the 1920s. As I remember the front room of a house had been converted into a surgery and all round the walls were posters depicting this or that disease in graphic detail. One in particular

The Black Bull, Warkworth, with Grandma Tully and Uncle Tommy, her son, who went on to be a police sergeant in Northumberland.

displaying the benefits of venereal disease were enough to make you faint. On a shelf out of reach there were some jars containing what appeared to be human specimens, but as I was about to investigate Stevo appeared in the doorway and crooked his finger. A scrawny man with a strong personality he took me into what was loosely termed his consulting room. Bare, a desk and chair, weighing machine and height measurer, the odd piece of paper and a stick with a rubber end which he used to tap my knees and elbows for reaction.

With a fag welded to his lips, a little grey nicotine stained tash and round glasses he looked just like Christie from Rillington Place. He ordered me to strip off to the buff, then piss in a jar … and there were no curtains. Gingerly I did his bidding then watched as he swilled my sample round like a fine wine, sniffed, then put a litmus tab into it.

'Is it all right?' I enquired nervously, attempting to look cool.

'You're not going to die,' said he tossing the sample into a sink in the corner. Well, at least that was something to be thankful for. After all he was an expert in pathology and putrefaction. Then he sprung it on me.

'Bend down.' I did so extremely reluctantly as he looked for something. Seemingly satisfied he ticked a box on a form then gave further instructions.

'Right boy up you get.' I looked quizzically. 'Up and down on the chair fifty times.'

'With nowt on?'

'I haven't all day boy,' and stood within inches as I hopped up and down like a nutcase, draughts everywhere. The yard of ash hung lower and lower as he started asking bloody silly questions. 'Ever had syphilis?'

'No.'

'Glandular fever?'

'No.'

'What about rhinitus?' Rhinitus? What the hell was that? It sounded like an affliction you could get if you were a young rhinoceros.

'Not that I know of.'

'Right, sit on the chair.' I was puffing like an old horse as he grabbed my wrist and stared at his pocket watch. The crafty old sod was after my pulse and recovery time.

'Okay get y'things on, nothing wrong a humane killer couldn't cure.'

He smiled … well I think it was a smile. A woman with a pram came up the path as I hastily dragged my kecks on, but I needn't have panicked because she never looked once, never mind twice.

A tale went round about old Stevo, who had a penchant for saving human tissue and one day, returning from a post mortem, left a diseased liver wrapped in newspaper on the rear seat of his car somewhere down Dean Street. His car was broken into and the parcel nicked, and every time Stevo referred to it he giggled at the thought of some unsuspecting cannibal eating his tea garnished with onions.

Next thing I was regurgitated onto the street with a clean bill of health. Medical passed with flying colours and to think it could all have been so different if I'd said I had rhinitus.

CARRIED INTO MANHOOD ON THE 'RED RATTLER'

Wharrier Street Cadet Training School in the East End of Newcastle. Big Jeff Hepworth, the instructor, disarms me on the judo mat while the others look on in glazed cadet apathy.

So, back to October 1959 and waiting for that damned bus. My uniform always felt awkward and uncomfortable, hairy, heavy material that soaked up moisture and smelled like an air raid shelter sand bag, while the musty flat caps always brought spots out on my brow. Valderma and Cuticura soap seemed to fester them even worse and my hair was always greasy despite constant washing. Blokes at the station reckoned if you wore the caps long enough they'd turn you bald.

You'd hear the bus first, coughing and spluttering, and had to peer into the foggy morning air to confirm it was a Newcastle 11 and not a Hunter's single decker heading you way. You couldn't be too careful, especially if the conductors winding arm was a bit lazy. I once jumped on the wrong one and ended up isolated and vulnerable in Wallsend High Street. You only ever went to Wallsend on a Saturday night, and then for a fight.

'Excuse me is this the eleven?' I don't know why I asked because there was never any reply. I found it difficult to compute that, here was me, a figure of authority and nobody taking a blind bit of notice. It took a long time to turn that frustration into positive and objective energy. An old copper once told me to remember the public need protecting despite themselves. He likened us to the 'midden men' as long as their shit was taken away in the dead of night they didn't care about where it was dumped as long as their netty was clean and fresh the following morning.

As the bus chugged closer, the queue would shrink and become urgent, prospective passengers girding their loins for a ceremonial boarding. Normally they would avoid physical contact, but when it was ten yards from the stop obscenity would prevail as they rubbed up and squashed against each other in panic for pole position. Nobody ever touched me, the uniform ensured absolute certain contagious immunity, but there were always loaded stares. Those looks which expected me to climb aboard last. After all, it was the decent thing to do, especially when it was assumed I wouldn't pay. Sometimes I did, sometimes not, but one thing for certain, I always had the money tucked in my glove at the ready.

Conductors came in all shapes and mental sizes. Some goose-stepped like the Gestapo, all slashed peaks and sewn into their drainpipes as if they were wired into the national grid screaming 'fares please' with grasping, dirty fingernails under my nose for maximum effect. Bloody embarrassing if you ain't got the dosh ready. Others, would take your money, pretend to click their machine and return the coin. The odd conductress would squeeze your hand and look you straight in the eye with a promise of … who knows what? I often got the feeling if I'd offered the money most of them would have been wounded deeply. None of the others passengers would notice, but I knew they all observed, because they recognised affinity in uniform. One guy would do conjuring tricks and pull the ticket from behind your ear. He was big and fat with lonely eyes and the sort of jollity which had grown organically as a protection against life. In those days the polis always rode shotgun for nowt. It was one of the perks, cos if a drunk or a worky ticket needed sorting it was done, no problem. Socially responsible back scratching. In our super sensitive world of political correctness, it would come heavily under the cloak of corruption now.

It was often a stumble up the winding stairs at the rear as the bus jerked away, accelerated, then inevitably crunched to a halt at the traffic lights. I never could get used to this ballet performance, double spin round the rear chromium handrail, then a plonking squeak onto the seat. Worse still, once at the destination, plummeting down metal steps on the moving vehicle like a sack of hammers made re-entry even more hazardous. I always hated that bloody boring journey. I was pig sick and wished I was on the job proper. Three years changing the Chief Constable's blotter, one of those rocking ones, collecting mail and fetching cigarettes for the Super, humping furniture and playing about with pay sheets was long enough for any man never mind an adolescent with postulating pimples.

One of my checkered highlights had been mistakenly buying the Super's cigarettes in packets of ten, instead of those round tins of fifties,

Spotty faced, innocent Cadets. With colleague Malcolm Young on the steps of the Old Town Hall – in the course of being office postmen. Malcolm went on to set up the Newcastle Drug Squad and then higher rank. He is now a respected academic on anthropology. Malcolm, an inspirational friend, doesn't realise that he was the first person to awaken me to the joy of writing when he showed me the book he was attempting to write.

and when I delivered them he slung them at my head. The Super? Big Sam, crafty sod used to leave his door ajar and myopically observe the office pond life sneaking up and down the passage through the crack. He looked remarkably like Fatty Arbuckle, star of the silent screen, and like him, I never actually heard him actually string a sentence together. The growl as he threw the ciggies at me did however communicate his feelings clearly.

I always endeavoured to perch on the outside of the rear seat of the bus, retaining the inside position for colleague Constable Johnny Weatherburn. Unless there was a three minute warning, I could guarantee that seat would remain vacant because nobody ever wanted to sit next to a copper, least of all a cadet! Only one bloke ever did and what a pain in the arse he was. A big wheezy old gadgy who'd been in the army and spoke in a loud voice asking personal questions.

'Just like the army eh?' What the hell was he on about?

'Going on watch eh son?' … 'How long you been on the force then eh?' … 'Good money is it?' … 'So where about's in Shields do y'live?'

On and bloody on he would go, it was purgatory as he breathed his mints all over me, waxed tash poked into my face. He looked like one of those toys which come to life in the loft at night. I'm told he was a prolific womaniser. If so he must have concentrated on Preston Park Blind School, or he had a big fat wallet.

Strange places buses, because temporarily everybody's on a time machine to destiny. The air was always thick with the offensive stench of Woodbines. I never could get used to it. Coughing, pale faced workers all poised pensively for the day ahead, each with private thoughts of whatever and waiting for their ten o'clock fix. Sickly sweet condensed milk tea to iron out the wrinkles as they sucked on double strength Capstan. There always seemed to be a joiner in overalls smelling of putty with a saw nodding dangerously from his haversack to become a focal hazard for everyone.

On this journey I learned the ancient art of eavesdropping on private conversations, enjoying their lives, hopes and dreams without jeopardy. Educating myself about the rhythms of conversation. I always watched the other passengers intently when I wasn't cogitating about Irene, the girl I was courting, or aggravation at home. The courting became a real problem as the months went on, especially for my mother. The rift between us became wider and lasted until I was well into my twenties and actually married which was always a sadness, but I loved Irene and was determined not to give her up. So these journeys away from home gave me valuable time for contemplative reflection. Another huge diversion was my now intense concentration on physical training and body building to aid my now continuing success in throwing the discus. I was undisputed Northumberland and Durham Champion in that and other events and began to dream of higher honours … maybe even representing my country. The blokes at work would laugh and ridicule me for that, but as time went on I made them eat their words.

Back to Johnny Weatherburn. He was a pleasant, kindly man and usually climbed on around Wills' Tobacco Factory. Always the same

With Irene and Irene's mother – bless her – outside Christ Church, North Shields. Irene had to go into debt big time for that coat. Irene's mam was a terrific source of support and strength to us both in extremely difficult times. She spent the bulk of her life up to her ankles in running water, gutting fish on North Shields Quay.

threadbare raincoat whatever the weather, tatty bait bag slung over his narrow shoulders and wisps of grey hair hanging limply on his collar. Johnny was dependable as time and just as relentless in his pursuit of it as he longed for retirement in a few short months. I wiped the window with the back of my leather gloves and my eyes scanned the bus stop. John wasn't there. Probably caught the bus in front. When I was a kid I could spit out the front window and it would re-enter the rear one as it caught the slipstream. Spitting seems to have played an important part of my former life.

Johnny was a nice old guy who spoke of nothing else but pottering at his caravan up at Beadnell in his high, quiet voice. He spoke of his wife who couldn't wait for his last shift to finish and often reflected on what she'd had to put up with as a copper's wife – it had been a career of its own and sometimes a tinge of bitterness crept into his tone. I often glanced at him from the corner of my eye during the long lulls in our conversation and wondered how he ever became a policeman.

He would sit for long periods nodding, mumming and smiling to himself. He looked dreadful, grey face, a slight stoop and hands which looked as if they never had any strength in them. He wouldn't hurt a fly poor bugger and had been on day shift light duties for years. An incessant cough was corroboration enough, but I could never fathom out why he smoked. His number was 430 – half past four! Daily I listened to his hopes for the future and he of mine, but I doubt he was really interested in me. My excitement to be sworn in as a fully fledged copper were matched pound for pound by his enthusiasm for retirement. It was a strange feeling, two cops in the same place and time, both eager in anticipation, but for entirely different reasons. A thirty year gap between us, yet it seemed but the blink of an eye.

He was usually very punctual, but it quickly left my mind. I was more interested in me. It never mattered which bus, some comedian had always rubbed the P off the 'No spitting' notice and substituted an H. Always confused me that, I mean if you're allowed not to, surely it must mean you can if you want to.

The last thirty six months as a police cadet had been frustrating, scuttling round Market Street police station watching regular constables who worked exciting shifts. Imperturbable giants with the skills to deal with catastrophes single handed. I longed to be like them, become involved in the nitty gritty, not having to visit the College of Commerce in Northumberland Road twice a week and being ordered to get my bloody hair cut every other day at the barbers in Shakespeare Street. No electric shears in there, it was clippers that stunk of oil and dragged the hair out in clumps. Why do barber's mirrors always make your face look like putty and your ears stick out?

A cold damp mist hung over the City Centre as I alighted in the Haymarket and had to dodge and weave through the cattle grids of the bus station. Walking that journey to the 'Nick' was always a bind because of the barrow boys polarising with their fly pitches at the junction of Northumberland Street and Prudhoe Street. Men of the world vending fruit and veg seconds to an eager public. Some of them almost romantic characters under pork pie hats making a backdrop for the little blue whisky veins on their ruddy faces. Providing a public service no doubt, but they gave me a hard time with a daily gypsy eyed onslaught.

'Cadet McKenzie, the long string of shite!' They would all laugh and smirk confidently.

'Look at him the prize puff.' I would rise to the bait like a mackerel to a feather, but could only offer violent verbiage in return.

'You talking to me?'

'He wants to know if we're talking to him lads?' and this would be followed by loud barking laughter pulling the hook tighter as they pushed their barrows into position for the day's obstruction, knowing I was powerless to act. Cadets were only pretend coppers, no teeth, baby gums, soft, lacking in bite. Nevertheless I would attempt to convince them I was the boss by stabbing my finger and puffing out my chest and on this day a warm two bob bit dropped from my glove and rang like Big Ben.

'I'll have you bastards, just wait and see.'

'Hear that lads? She's lost her temper now.' Members of the public would congregate as I became the floor show. Beetroot red in embarrassment and anger I hurried away and in my haste nearly knocked over a window cleaner's ladder up against the shoe shop. The man on the top of his shaky perch vented a mouthful of abuse and it felt the whole world was looking.

'Sorry pal.' What else could I say? Angry and frustrated as the laughs increased from the hyenas behind I strode off beetroot red.

Northumberland Street teemed with life at that time in the morning, and you could tell if you were early or pushed for time by the position of regulars. One or two smart things, but not that many. The most interesting were the pseudo business men, young lads out to impress. By their numbers and the way they dressed it seemed that they must have been spawned like young smolt, from in behind Burtons the tailors. A road sweeper bounced his way up the gutter, brush darting, refuse springing ahead. He nodded in recognition, same affinity as the bus conductress, probably thought he was important cos he knew the polis … looked a cracker if the truth really be told.

The big city had a different smell to Shields which stunk most days of the Guano Fish Works as it spewed its filthy muck into the atmosphere. But Newcastle exuded the scent of bread shops, exhaust fumes and coffee shops. The noises were different also, the people all looked as if they were going somewhere important and you had this feeling of anonymity. There was always an army of chamois men polishing the large sheets of glass with a makeshift pole with a strip of leather attached, complete with bucket of dirty steaming vinegar water. Other gauntlets had to be run, accidents, collapses and the occasional shopkeeper who demanded I did something about the tramp who slept at the rear of Fenwicks. I had to tell him in gentle tones that I had no intention of taking the flea bitten rat bag home.

The Police Station building loomed nearer, a sanctuary, a large stone refuge on the corner of Pilgrim Street and Market Street, incorporating the courts, with impressive revolving doors more befitting a luxury hotel. Attached to it by a concrete umbilical was the magnificent fire station and they shared a communal yard. Through the archway into this inner sanctum fire engines were polished waver thin by shirt sleeved firemen with ant like intensity. Station officers would bark commands like army drill sergeants, a performance I would often

I doubt if there is anyone who served in the police in the Newcastle area in the 1960s and '70s who cannot relate some story about Arthur McKenzie. The difficulty lies in the absolute fact that Arthur was, and still is, larger than life.

In 1963, as a young constable of nineteen, whose only claim to fame was to be among the smallest recruits to have joined the Newcastle City Police, PC McKenzie was indeed my hero. It was not just that he was among the biggest, strongest and fittest man I ever met. He was also one of the funniest and enthusiastic people to be with. Duty became fun. He was a prolific thief taker, a skill he honed simply by having an unquenchable curiosity and the gift of lateral thought. He was an excellent, practical police officer and a fine leader of men.

Sadly, the Service lost him whilst he still had plenty to offer. But that is also to our advantage, as one of Arthur's talents is that of raconteur, often against himself. Having witnessed a small part of his many exploits, I just know that what he writes is the truth, the whole truth and probably nothing like the truth some of his colleagues would care to recall.

Gavin Aarvold, Chief Superintendent (Retired)

watch from the court office window marvelling as the turntable ladder shot skywards, nodding in the wind, high above the city a fireman perilously clinging to it.

The revolving doors slattered and clattered propelling me into another smell area ... floor polish! Walking down the passage there were high desks right and left with an odd glance from those engrossed in paper work. Glass partitions everywhere, hiding paper generals, assiduously driving their desks – but there was always the excitement of the unknown. Frank Mavin, one of the cadets once arrested a guy for murder – well he actually gave himself up at the counter, but it was still a good case and all of a sudden we all got a whiff of the excitement. A typical West End tenement strangling. Burglar looking for the mattress money, wakes the old biddy up and croaks her. Sad, and the last case in Newcastle where the judge put on the black cap and sentenced him to death ... I watched the trial ... very eerie ... but the sentence was commuted and he was out after a few years and back to thieving – so much the price of a life!

The police station was self contained, all departments and officers in close proximity, everyone's antecedents for public consumption, no secrets, a pecking order definitely existed. I headed towards the Chief Constable's administration department where I was currently working. Within reach of the revolving doors my role was to attend to the public like an encyclopaedia salesman. The Chief's Office was where all the bright boys gravitated, men identified for leadership qualities cocooned and groomed for the future. A rare species to be protected, always immaculate and looking for the main chance to catch the gaffer's eye. Once ensconced, promotion was more or less guaranteed. Truth of the matter was most were there because of family contacts, freemasons, attended the right church or members of the police choir. Of course there was the odd good guy, but by and large nepotism was alive and kicking hard in the late fifties. In contrast to real coppers they always smelled of shaving soap with thoughts of only one thing – promotion.

In those innocent days I didn't have a clue about such things, for my real attention was on the bleary eyed monoliths drifting down the waxed passage, intent on refreshments or preparing for a further spell on the patch. Some still unshaven, but men of action with magical stories about catching this prig or that pudden eater. Fighting in the Bigg Market, locking up a burglar or, even better, a safe blower. One man did however stand head and shoulders above the rest, the man who had drawn me into the job. George Bone, storeman extraordinaire. A Yorkshireman with a mind like Sheffield steel, I swear he paid for the gear himself and would have made a terrific Chancellor. George was near to the end of his career, and probably the only one in the department without any ambition whatsoever ... except to save money. A large rotund individual, balding with a smile like a grave digger looking for a tip. Teeth false, enamel dazzle with an uncontrollable click and set slightly at an angle. The few strands of hair he thought he had looked as if they'd been painted on with brylcream and invariably a dob would dangle off his ear. I can hear him now as he picked up the phone and slid into posh Yorkshire/Geordie – wonderful!

'Ello, Queen Mary here, I wonder if you could give me a quote to have the barnacles scraped off my bottom?' The conversation would continue. 'That requisition for more accident books, well you'll have to wait to the end of the month, sorry.' The smile posing as a grimace would remain switched on his face, but not in his mind as he clattered the phone down.

'They take 'em home for the kids to crayon in, must think I'm stupid,' and would then disappear along the passage in a rolling gate, head on one side like a blackbird looking for a worm, then down the stairs into his cubby hole. Alladin's cave was a more apt description, it was festooned with uniforms, badges, buttons, capes, helmets and caps and every one was ceremoniously accounted for, they were like his children, his family in blue serge. No one ever extricated from George anything to which he wasn't entitled and he could wipe the snarl off a rottweiler at fifty paces if you merely hinted your interest in a garment.

George had a partner in crime. Old Walter, a bent wizened man of seventy who wheezed like a set of bellows and constantly had a length of ash dripping from one corner of his mouth and was laughably called the tailor. Crouched over his sewing machine in one corner his chest heaved like a pigeon cree. Tweedle Dum and Tweedle Dee, they didn't have to speak, their non verbals were clear. 'What do you want?' … 'Sign for it and 'Get out!'

Back upstairs in the Chief's office the cadet's job was really just to fetch and carry, file and say sir all the time. First job was to sort out the mail and enter every letter in the huge correspondence ledger, and what a performance that was. A pen and ink job then, nibs that squeaked on the paper then sprang like steel traps spraying everywhere and powdered ink you had to mix by the gallon. I did have a stroke of luck early on whilst attached to this office. It was one quiet mid afternoon and during lunch I'd gone to buy my Health and Strength magazine and was hunched and engrossed over pictures of Reg Park and Steve Reeves, digesting their routines, when a voice shook me from my imagination.

'What's that you're reading?' I turned and immediately jumped to attention for there looking over his glasses was George Jackson, the Chief Constable no less. A kindly, stooped man he smiled before I could reply and lifted the magazine.

'Bit of a fitness fanatic are you McKenzie?'

'Yes sir.'

'Right then son, come with me,' and he led me along the passage to his office at the end. Once inside he shut the door, took off his jacket, rolled his sleeves up and pointed to a fifty six pound potato weight on the floor.

'Six each arm, okay?' and to my amazement this outwardly frail, elderly man lifted the weight and pressed it full height each arm without any bother at all then indicated.

'Right let's see what you can do.' I got it up but could only manage four with my right and three with my left.

Training in the yard at Wharrier Street Cadet Training School in the East End of Newcastle at 16.

At Gateshead as a callow discus thrower with 'bumpers and socks to die for'.

'Okay son, every day I expect you to do four reps each arm after you've changed my blotter.' Incredibly, over a period of months I managed to progress to twelve each arm which was a terrific boost to my confidence and eradicated much of the boredom of playing with paper and filing.

Once the early morning settled and staff drifted off into their various departments with pieces of paper everyone became secure in their individual territories and hum drum set in. Beat men would come in for their bait, rain on their capes and half shaved through being on earlies and oh, how I envied them. On the streets there was live action, the nearest the conversation ever got to police work in the office was a heady discussion about the Annual Police Ball and how the Deputy Chief had once chased a cop at the Old Assembly Rooms and burst his balloon. Villains tearing the arse out of the town would have trembled in their balaclavas had they known. Even the typists were boring, sitting upright, superior in their fifty words a minute without looking at the keys. The odd smile or nod and maybe a glimpse of a brogue or, if you were really lucky, a heavily wrapped surgical stocking.

The office clock pointers would stutter towards the witching hour. Once it hit ten o'clock there was a mass exodus to the canteen and you were nearly killed in the stampede. It was the same at five o'clock as the Pavlov's dogs fought their way out to oblivion into the streets to scramble onto buses and trains before dark – aspiring to high rank must have been very stressful.

The canteen lay right in the bowels, within a stone's throw of the cell block, lavatories and photographic department. Managed by the infamous Miss Bankhead one look from her would wither, and a smile? – well that could destroy any living creature. Her tea had the potential to bring your braces down through flared nostrils and her culinary resistance were her surprise scones. Consisting nine parts bicarbonate of soda and one part salt, they would fizz and pop in your mouth destroying the taste buds in double quick time, then rift up for the rest of the day and often revisit you in bed. Tallula, as we called her, had a sidekick, a young girl slightly short of sand with suppurating scabs on her lips. She was hard working and well meaning, but her customer care left a little to be desired. I happened upon her once eagerly sucking the savoury crusts from sauce bottle tops with relish. According to her she was 'cleaning them'. My stomach turned over like knotty porridge and I've never used sauce since and neither has my daughter after I relayed this little nugget to her. I had this recurring nightmare of collapsing in the canteen with scone poisoning then she would set about reviving me with mouth to mouth!

Despite having to run this gastronomic gauntlet every day the break gave an opportunity to meet up with the other cadets sprinkled within the departments. On this day in question the canteen was packed to capacity with non combatants nodding and laughing at the bosses' jokes. The cadets had a non threatening table near to the back wall. I attacked my scone from the rear to take it by surprise. There was an atmosphere mingled in with the fried sausage. Everyone gabbling in animated tones on the same subject.

'Have you heard about Johnny Weatherburn?'

'No, what?' My senses razor sharp despite the explosions in my mouth.

'Poor old sod's been reported missing from home.' Brian knew all the gossip first because he was working in the information room.

'Aye, went out with his dog, never came back. They reckon he's gone mad.' I was shocked and excited at the same time. The topic of conversation then homed in on madness and its relevance to those working in the various offices. Poor old Johnny was nothing more than a nine second wonder. There were other important things to think about. Pay parade, annual leave coming up, or even better a bit of special duty at the football match. Cynical bastards, coppers, the holocaust would just be recorded as another incident.

Madness? I suppose the euphemism would now be stress, but it all boils down to the same thing in the end ... gossip! Yes! There were more than a few borderline cases about. I once saw a detective throw a typewriter through a window into Pilgrim Street because somebody else, and not him, had been promoted. There was definitely a touch of madness about him. One minute he'd be laughing, the next staring into space and striding from the office growling like a dog. Then the admin detective sergeant, who looked like Bob Hope, spent most of his day farting and smiling as the office cleared around him. Yes characters abounded, it was a marvellous period.

The Court Office was another clearing house for the insane where peculiar people who hung like cobwebs from every desk. Like the rest of the station the desks were high and the stools even higher ... a total throwback to Dickens. Nicknamed 'Harmony Hall' there were about eight working there all with that wide eyed look which was probably caused through too many scones and tea. One poor guy had a breakdown and had to be pulled off the window sill trying to top himself. The Superintendent in charge, Bob Whalton was a cracking bloke and his loud booming baritone voice could often be heard singing Gilbert and Sullivan from his office. A man's man he would shout at you, but with a glint in his eye and often called me in to give me tickets for a rugby match. He later went on to become Chief Constable of Hull and was a big miss to the force.

One afternoon I found myself alone with one man. Half past three and I'm staring at PC Arthur Grimes from Hull. A stocky, rough and ready individual with a shock of dark hair and a personality to match. His uniform was always unkempt and birds could have nested in the stubble on his face.

'Don't make the same mistakes I did son.' He gripped my hand firmly.

'Where are you going? What's the matter?' I was mystified.

'It's my last day son. See those bastards I work with, they've slithered off like snakes cos they didn't want to say tara. Well who needs them?' And flung open the glass door hoofing his cap along the passage singing 'Cumberland Gap' at the top of his voice. He walked from the job his own man, beholden to no one ... no ACC giving a eulogy at the police club, where the wife gets flowers and chocolates and the cop a teasmade – if he is lucky.

Anyway, I couldn't help thinking about poor old John. Yes, he hadn't been on the bus and yes, he was missing from home. I just hoped he was all right. Time passed, the day ended and I was back on Northumberland Street heading for home, another day over. Thank God it wasn't going to be for much longer, very soon I was going to be sworn in but I couldn't get poor old John out of my mind. Missing from home? It didn't seem possible, surely they would see his dog? Two days later news came through and strangely enough it wasn't a shock. John had been discovered dead, a heart attack behind Wills' Tobacco Factory on the Coast Road, his body in the long grass. Madness never entered into it. I was upset about him in a distant sort of way, but life had to go on. His dog? Probably handed into the cat and dog shelter. Could have been given a good home I suppose, but no doubt it ended up dancing on the electric plate. Wills' building has now been converted into luxury flats! Every time I pass I think of John who never got to retire to his caravan up at Beadnell. An ordinary man, living out his ordinary life, but his existence motivated me to grasp every opportunity with both hands.

'I AM NOT A NUMBER, I AM A FREE MAN' ... 'LIKE HELL I WAS'

Taken outside the garage at Newby Wiske Hall Training School – a fearsome sight I do declare. I look as if I'm going to be shot.

D day arrived, 18th December 1958, the journey to Newcastle was fun as all my thoughts concentrated on my emergence from this cadet chrysalis as a full blown brightly plumaged copper. Life was to change dramatically in the next few hours! One thing the police force offered above all else was variety, if I'd had to end up in an office job it would have killed me. There was a spring in my step that frosty morning when I breezed through the revolving doors of the police station in my best suit. Somehow the other cadets looked younger and I hadn't even been sworn in yet. I had been told to wait in the canteen until called. Trapped with three other innocents, we were captives, the four of us sitting uncomfortably in opposite formation. We all played with Talulla's powerful tea, hands nervously rubbing the well worn formica topped table, making chit chat talk. Our antecedents spilled out: shipyards, army, train driver, my three partners in crime had all seen the big wide world and were so much older than me. In their late twenties, married with that look of life experience etched on their faces. I was a boy in their midst, yet for some reason they thought because I'd been stumbling blindly round the station for nearly three years I held all the secrets.

The ubiquitous George Bone stuck his head round the door and summoned us forth with a flick of his ample, well practised neck. Quickly, we proceeded to the stairwell where George had the lift jammed open with a large ledger. He knew all the dodges. Only a week previous a civvie had staggered into the side door from Market Street, had an epileptic fit and fallen on top of me down those same steps. The thoughts that flitter through your mind in moments of stress. The atmosphere was claustrophobic as we glanced at each other in anticipation, about to blast off into a destination unknown.

The antediluvian lift had criss cross concertina gates outer and inner, which had to be clashed shut. George switched on the power, carefully controlled the handle and it slowly jerked its way to the Courts landing, two floors up. Halting it at the correct level depended totally on accurate precision of hand and eye co-ordination and if you overshot your destination you were trapped until the mechanics were called. George hummed 'The Man from Laramie' a fixed satanic grin, displaying a concentration which indicated real business. The situation was almost ritualistic. I remember thinking how smart he looked, an old soldier … 'bull-shit baffles brains.' It was if I had been chewing mescaline, everything was in slow motion, George, his large, secret book clutched tightly under his arm. Suddenly realisation hit home that this ceremony had real meaning, and George's sombre mood was catching. None of us spoke, the odd twitch of a smile, but our faces stayed pale and drained.

Like a swan with its cygnets George led us into Court Number One, an old-style place fitted with mahogany majesty and an atmosphere akin to a church. George contained us with his meaty arm at the rear near the double doors as the court was full and business was as usual. The public gallery was full of rubber neckers, associates, friends of the accused and a children's school party. Some poor drunk was dispatched down the stairs from the dock and the Magistrates Clerk, F. Morton Smith, indicated George move us to the front. We filed into the front bench reserved for prosecution and defence solicitors who bunked along to let us in. F. Morton Smith indicated we sit and we responded like obedient children. Suddenly there was a knock on wood, the clerk demanded we all 'Stand up' and from behind the high backed magisterial chairs a door opened, two local beaks walked in, sat down and looked condescendingly at us – four sacrificial rookies on the altar of Justice.

George stood ramrod and spoke to the court in an extremely refined Geordie voice, informing 'their worships' that we were to be sworn in, attested as constables. Dutifully he handed over magic documents and the secret book which was signed by the magistrates and countersigned by the clerk. George leaned forward confidentially to Morton Smith and they became engrossed in jabbering and whispering. We were then each handed a card and asked to repeat the printed affirmation in unison. Like four parrots we swore allegiance to God and the Queen without fear or favour. The muttering in the public gallery heightened our self consciousness to the grave proceedings, but somehow we struggled through. I was most certainly hot under the collar, then the senior magistrate welcomed us in words mechanical, no heart and completely repetitious, to uphold the law, protect the public peace and he hoped we would all have illustrious careers. It was so obvious he had performed this onerous task so many times before his wishes of good luck sounded hollow. I suppose this was the first real indicator of the harshness of the real world and that we were only a small part of an enormous sausage machine. Task completed George wheeled us past the rubbernecking public, into the shaky lift and down into Aladdin's cave.

Old Walter, the tailor, looked dreadful, but had sorted a batch of uniforms for us. He never spoke, only grunted and despite the fact I'd been in and out of the place for a couple of years he never acknowledged me in any shape or form. For the next hour and a half we were supplied with uniform by the ton and hardly any of it new. The hats were hermetically sealed in brown paper bags and once that seal was broken the hat was yours, even if it was two sizes too big. The trick then would be to fold a piece of cardboard and tuck it into the leather inner rim to make it fit until your head grew into it. As the years rolled on it was far easier to let your hair grow.

George's recycling process involved a 'fitting where it touched' principle and most of my kit left enough room for at least another two cops.

'Try this on.' An overcoat was hoisted into position by three of them. Its weight dragged my shoulders down and the length convinced me we were going to perform duty in the Russian Steppes. On top of the jumper, tunic, shirt and trousers I felt like some ungainly monster lumbering up and down the passage. A practice run to be a human battering ram.

'Yes porfect fit son, you'll soon take up the slack with a few hot pies in you.' I know I was green, but despite George's persuasion, I could detect his meaty hands clasping a yard of material at the back. As far as he was concerned there was a whole career's worth of wear in it yet, some more old uniform discarded. He would have done the Chancellor proud.

Some of the kit was that musty you'd have been forgiven if it had seen out the Relief of Mafeking, and distribution was a lost art. 'Grab, hoi, here y'are son, this looks like a nice one.' And if you touched it, or better still if it touched you it was yours. Sidling over to try and persuade old Walter to make alterations, like taking feet off the hem, forget it. That was like asking for blood and by the looks of him there wasn't too much of that left. Now I knew why coppers were always dodging into cafes and pubs. It was necessary to build themselves up to fit their bloody uniforms.

Staggering away under box loads of hairy blue serge, truncheon and snips I headed for the billiard room above the garage in the yard. In the silence and subdued lighting I had the onerous task of fixing my numbers in my epaulettes. Up until now I had been carried along on a quarter-master-stores syndrome of acceptance and signatures. The monasterial tranquillity of the snooker room seemed to shut me completely off from the outside world. I was able to gather my thoughts and had half an hour till lunch. I had a grand plan of action, but first I must get the numbers in. Chromium digits tumbled from the envelope and I sorted them into pairs, along with the split pins to secure them. Suddenly I realised my number had a ring about it '430' half past four! Four o'clock half struck! Then it hit me – I had been given old John's number. I shivered, my pal John who I'd sat next to all those months listening, his numbers inches from my own shoulders. It was uncanny, as if, in some way, I had represented the angel of death, waiting patiently for those numbers he had carried proudly for nearly thirty years. The silence in the billiard room added to the atmosphere and I wondered for one eerie moment if he was watching me. I couldn't get him out of my mind as I hacked the epaulettes with a sharp knife and inserted my own personality.

A strange transformation takes place once you become a number. An anonymity which separates you from being a real person, a bar-code to be inserted into football details and duty rosters. It gives power-crazy supervisors the right to scream and belittle you as they hide behind their rank. It also provides swift identification to the public in order they can complain with ease. What a simple idea numbers are, they take the pressure off the system. As I sat in the corner of the billiard room I promised myself I was going to try and retain my identity. Arthur McKenzie was a human being. Finishing my blue serge bingo I struggled into my tunic. The rest of the day was mine and I had things on my mind.

* * * * * * * * * * * * * * * * * * * *

'Every man should know his own limitations.'
Clint Eastwood

Plan A commenced the moment I stepped through the archway into Pilgrim Street. I stood and surveyed the big wide world which was now to be my oyster. I had only one thought, and striding up Northumberland Street had my fingers tightly crossed that I wouldn't be called upon to deal with an accident. My eyes searched. Barrow Boys! Yes! There they were, and still think I'm a cadet. As I approached they made no attempt to move, faces wreathed in smiles, but the public sensed all was not well and shied away. I watched for several delicious moments then steeled myself against the tirade which was bound to come. I spat out the words.

'Right, names and addresses?' They took no notice and continued to laugh and peddle their wares. I stepped forward with gusto and confronted them, numbers shining like diamonds on my shoulders.

'Names and addresses NOW,' I demanded. The world stopped and their expressions of defiance changed as they spotted the glinting digits.

'Ah, come on mister McKenzie, give us a chance, we've just come out.' So now it was mister McKenzie? I smiled and withdrew my pocket book which felt like a newly baked bun in my hand. From the corner of my eye I could see their 'lookouts' sliding away, but I had the main protagonists trapped. No going back now and my prey looked as sick as chips. The pocket book pages were crisp and I had to bend the seam hard to stop them springing closed.

'You're going six and eights mister McKenzie. I mean, howay, we've all got to make a living. Want some mushrooms?' They pleaded like sulking kids and for a few seconds I actually felt sorry for them, but the moment soon passed.

'Ah come on man, don't let it get personal, can you not take a joke?'
'Am I laughing?'
'Live and let live mister McKenzie … we knew you were going to go far.' I savoured the moment, but if the truth be known I didn't really quite know what I was doing, or how to handle it, trembling slightly as

Marching with my fellow cadets at Wharrier Street in 1957. Included are: Bill Taylor, Brian Taylor, Frank Mavin, John Patterson, Bill Galstone, Mick Potts. John Thompson, John Bensley and Brian Jackson.

I wrote. Fortunately they didn't notice.

Revenge was sweet, and the barrow boys and I had nearly ten years courtship, eventually learning to live with each other. They knew if I caught them a summons was inevitable, but by the same token would often turn a blind eye provided they moved when they saw me. It was really all about mutual respect. A moment of pure ecstasy, but short lived as I learned to recognise that in fact they were harmless and only trying to make a few bob.

All hell let loose when I returned to the police station twenty minutes later. 'Fergie' the station sergeant bollocked me up hill and down dale. One of the barrow boys had telephoned ahead with a complaint.

'Who do you think you are? A knight on a white horse?'

'But they were causing obstruction sergeant.'

'Listen kid, you better get this in your noddle and quick. This is a disciplined service and you don't go round doing what YOU think is right. Y'book here,' and snatched it from me testily. In bold strokes he struck out the entry I had so lovingly made. He obliterated everything with the words: 'In error. PC McKenzie has been warned as to further behaviour and has been cautioned by me.' He then signed it with a flourish and thrust it back into my hand. Inside I was boiling, and about to retaliate, but he must have seen my eyes flashing.

'Don't even think about it son, you haven't had the puddens. Now go and get me twenty ciggies at Stan Seymour's.'

'Sorry sergeant,' and he looked at the numbers on my shoulder.

'You'd better get a cadet.' I stood firm and he stood and looked at me smouldering, then turned and walked off extremely angry indeed. I certainly hadn't made a friend, maybe I'd won a round, but little did I know that he and I would have a long battle of attrition, with many blows from both sides.

I returned to the canteen to lick my wounds, joining the others. We all had rookie stamped on our foreheads, each wondering what lay ahead, feeling self conscious in our new-for-old uniforms. Fishes gasping on the bank, it seemed the only place prepared to breathe life into us was the training school and I was looking forward to that like a hole in the head. The system had the last word. George Bone stopped me in the passage.

'Pocket book laddie,' hand outstretched, flapping towards his body.

'What for George?' I knew fine well, but intended to assert myself.

'Do you want the super to know he's just signed on an idiot?'

'You mean the sergeant hasn't already told him?' He grabbed me by the front of my tunic with alarming speed, teeth clacking in my face, breath smelling of bacon and egg.

'Do you want to taste hospital food kid?' Reluctantly I handed my pocket book over.

'Do that again I'll make you pay for the next one,' said George as he made me sign for a new one.

It was a long time before I realised the significance of what had happened. Fergie had been totally out of line to cancel a perfectly good summons and realising he had acted hastily and, picking up on my anti attitude, knew it might be embarrassing. Several years later I found out this particular barrow boy had been one of Fergie's snouts calling in his marker. Fergie had been forced to respond and covered his tracks nicely, a shrewd man who was to ride me like a cowboy for years, but it gives a flavour of the job as it was then. Every day a new experience, another lesson learned. It also has to be said that even though I had been sworn in, legally I had no real authority until I'd been to the training school, so I was clearly out of order.

* * * * * * * * * * * * * * * * * * *

From boy into man in thirteen weeks …
Who's kidding who?

Two days into 1959 found me staggering up the gravel drive of the Number 2 District Training School Newby Wiske, near Northallerton in Yorkshire like an evacuee. One foot in the past, one in the present and hovering over an uncertain future made me feel extremely vulnerable. Cadet life of being a pretend policeman quickly melted into the past, but another demon had now taken its place, because training school encapsulated everything I hated. Petty-fogging regulations, living away from home and coming to terms with real life as I was being subjected to discipline and forced to grow up. This isolated, baronial hall, set in beautiful surroundings became my home for thirteen weeks, and I detested it intensely. Only at the weekends could I return home to a proper bed and grub.

Recruits wandered aimlessly as if hypnotised, muttering definitions and powers of arrest. Parrots of law, everything learned along those lines and we could recite huge sections from Moriarty (the Police Bible of law which had more weight than the Commandments), but understand it? Highly debatable. The more zealous instructors would often leap unsuspectingly from behind a tree in the grounds and confront us with. 'Name me sixteen offences under the Town Police Clauses Act?' and as you stammered through legalistic mumbo jumbo, other recruits would beetle past, hearts in their mouths, thankful for their good fortune.

The food was deplorable. To call it pig-swill would be a compliment. Anaemic peas ran into watery mince which smelled of soap and the remnants of yesterday's meal on knives and forks were testament to its indigestibility. Each weekend I would stagger up the drive on my return, suitcase packed with sustenance, pies, nuts, crisps, fruit and sandwiches.

My stay there was one horrible dream, interminably saluting the instructors who strutted like bloody chocolate soldiers and we were quickly reduced to a level below that of children and rarely treated like men. The Commandant, nicknamed the 'Black Prince' was a miserable bugger who stalked about in a neck brace and followed everywhere like a lap dog by his deputy superintendent, a gentle old soul, who sucked a pipe and wouldn't say boo to a goose, but the Black Prince thought he was running Colditz.

It was a particularly severe winter and George Bone must have been looking into his crystal ball because the seven ton overcoat came in very useful. The accommodation was so cold we even started looking forward to drill in order to keep warm. So, as the weeks passed, we were trapped, prisoners in a location more frightening than any Hammer Production movie. The mist constantly hung suspended two feet off the ground, and a long crunching drive lined with thickets of large trees made the grounds eerie. Knotty-barked pines creaked and groaned constantly in the night reminding us of their power and secrets.

The Hall had been split up into dormitories and I was on the first floor next to the broad winding staircase. The room housed six of us and every day we had to box our blankets and stand by our beds for inspection. It was a cheerless room with cold lino on the floor and the beds were army style, basic metal frames with thin mattresses. During the hours of darkness all that could be heard was the 'tock-tock' of a grandfather clock as it maintained the beat of the night. This wooden box of cogs, half way up the oak staircase, would chime at odd times. Well, clunked is a better description. It got right on your nerves and I would pray someone would mend it or chop the bloody thing up for firewood!

Strong rumours circulated that two suicides had occurred there many years earlier. The old classics, I suppose, a master putting one of the maids in the family way and they both had topped themselves, she by hanging and he hurling himself from the roof. There was in fact one room boarded up at one end of our dorm and the atmosphere at times was real and not imagined. Apparently a couple of years earlier strange happenings had reached fever pitch necessitating a priest to be called to exorcise the building. Of course full of bravado everyone used to kid on about it, but privately I always had a strange feeling in the pit of my stomach.

One night the uncanny did happen when I was awakened by a high shrill scream of terror. The recruit who occupied the bed opposite to me was sitting bolt upright, ashen white, mortally terrified. 'There's a head floating above your bed.' I didn't have to be told twice and my next steps were bloody big ones and spent the remaining night hours learning definitions in the lounge. Resident members of staff would get blind drunk at weekends to make life tolerable, or that was the excuse given, but they all were convinced the place was haunted. No doubt about it, Newby Wiske was a phantom's dream, dark passages, strange noises and a willing, captive audience.

It was also circulated that the authorities added bromide to the tea, but from the antics of the instructors, canteen and cleaning staff it would seem their brew came from another pot. In corners, confidential conversations described moonlight walks to the sewerage farm with some nurse or another. Many a young copper met his future spouse at the weekly dance held on the premises. Conversely many a marriage was poisoned.

Training school was a total anathema to me because I had always resisted discipline, but I had to take the forced feeding on judicial porridge and regimented programme. The bulk of us had thoughts of only one thing, to escape from this play acting in order to commence implementation of every piece of legislation lodged in our little brains. Crisp, staccato, we knew most of it backwards, little realising it was to be the only way of enforcement on occasions. I did however warm to our syndicate instructor, Sergeant James, who turned out to be a first class teacher and honest individual … rather against the grain compared to the rest of them. He went on to become a Deputy Chief I believe and then one of the first ever heart transplant patients at the Freeman Hospital in Newcastle.

There was a plus side and one of the recruits who had joined with me, Jimmy Lawson, persuaded me to learn to drive in the grounds of the school. He owned a really old sit up and beg Ford and during lunch breaks patiently put me through my paces and suggested that I should apply for a driving test cancellation. By sheer luck I got the letter a couple of weeks later and panic set in. Fortunately the date of my test coincided with one of our few long weekends so Jim forced me to drive the car home on the Friday morning and straight into the test at Osborne Road. Incredibly I performed my emergency stops and three point turns without mishap and passed first time. What a wonderful sense of achievement for which I will always be in debt to Jim.

By the time thirteen weeks was up I had been boxed into shape, and thoughts of pass out were sweet. I worked hard and came joint second top and received a glowing report which was a feather in their cap bearing in mind my school experience. I have to say the march past and inspection on that last day was a proud one, our syndicate 209 was extremely smart, there was a sense of achievement and we'd all become old sweats. Within days of return to the force however realisation dawned. We had only been play acting and the chasm between theory and practice an enormous divide which could only be spanned with time and experience. Practical exercises at the school always ended as neat tidy parcels, everything done and dusted, pocket book entries spot on and station procedures exactly right. Real-life situations established this as the exception rather than the rule with day to day events staggering along from crisis to crisis. Our calculated pavlovian academic requirements plus response of the past thirteen weeks were now replaced with uncertainty, danger and the unexpected lurking around every corner. No time for poltergeists, these were now going to be real life situations.

Syndicate 209 Newby Wiske Training School. Note we all have clenched fists ready for the white knuckle ride into the Bigg Market. In the front row, either side of Sergeant James (one of the first long-surviving heart transplant patients at the Freeman Hospital, Newcastle) are Newcastle men. Left to right: John Henderson, myself, Norman Dawson, Bob Charlton (who tragically died not long after), Jimmy Lawson (who taught me to drive in three weeks) and Doug Hudson.

SECTION FOUR

THERE ARE A MILLION STORIES IN THE BIG CITY

Night shift is the only one where real police work is executed and my first touring Divisions was a baptism of fire. Newcastle West End was notorious for its toughness, slums, crime, prostitution, dirt and degradation. Like many other depressed areas it derived this reputation from pockets of such activity which created ghettos of crime and unfortunately the whole district was then tarred with the same brush. My first duty fell on a Friday night, and at nine thirty I reported as a fresh faced, bright eyed and bushy-tailed enthusiast to the Cattle Market Section House. Located on the infamous Scotswood Road slap bang in the centre of market pens, it consisted of a rat infested hut adjoining the killing shops. The stench of bile, saturated sawdust and death permeated the entire structure. If animals possess souls this building must have been well overcrowded. It's amazing that this same site now houses the Centre For Life built on a centre of death which in turn was erected on a centre of life and death (a hospital).

The cops who worked those bottom beats, the 'hard end', reported for and terminated duty from this hut which also adjoined the Central Division. So it became a meeting place for the two divisions where information, bait and card schools could be shared. A section sergeant would occasionally parade the shift then during the course of a shift drop on staff unexpectedly in their supervisory role. Some were right sneaky bastards and attempt to catch you out, but the bulk were fair minded men who really wanted a quiet life and the opportunity to pursue their own assignations. The telephone operator was a key man as all messages and incidents were relayed through him and you would have to ring in every hour and often they would keep you informed as to where the enemy was. Appointments with supervision, both

Cattle Market, N C on Tyne. (142)

The noises, smells and sheer frenzy of the Cattle Market where often a bull would escape and create mayhem as it rampaged through the city. One once managed to be trapped in St James' Park – but a marksman shot it before it could be signed on.

sergeant and inspector would be usually made around ringing times at the few boxes and pillars scattered within the division, the classic 'Tardis', wonderful places of respite where many a snooze was performed.

On this night however there was no sergeant and from the looks on the faces of the older men it was obvious I was a liability, for showing round a probationer was akin to carrying a bag of coal. As far as they were concerned 'lock ins' called, but fortunately a cop whom I'd known as a cadet, Billy Warnes, readily agreed I team up with him. The others must have sighed with relief. Bill was a good lad and bloody good footballer and cricketer, so with my sporting bent he and I had a common thread of conversation. Apart from that, even though he didn't have a great deal of service his reputation as a good polis went ahead of him. He knew his patch like the back of his hand and was consistently locking up thieves. I felt easy in his company, especially after hearing tales of older coppers forcing recruits to walk in the gutter. A lot of the old sweats had seen action during the war so their attitude was uncompromising. Us young-uns were seen as soft.

'The job's not what it used to be … it's knackered,' is the cry successive generations bemoan. 'T.J.F'd' is another common expression.

Stepping into the crisp night air I suddenly felt vulnerable, but excited, having waited for that moment ever since George Bone had given me my numbers. Everything was drab in the half sodium lights and within minutes we were flitting shadows in a different world. Bill worked two beat – the boundaries of Scotswood Road, Marlborough Crescent, up Westgate road, back down Elswick Road and through the streets down to Scotswood again. Friday nights on the 'bottom end' were always hairy and I marvelled as Bill with his south country accent moved on obnoxious drunks and prostitutes, like a sheepdog herding his flock. Had it been me I would have been making arrests every time a voice was raised, but Bill's calm, careful approach taught me an important early lesson in tolerance.

'Always check the backs first 'cos cows take their punters there and their pimps roll them. No good finding a body on your patch at four in the morning which could have been lying there since half past ten. Clear your hot spots first quick as possible.' Bill walked fast, occasionally doubling back unexpectedly, every dodgy lock and door known intimately. It was fascinating, dark, thrilling, even though nothing of note occurred. Nothing that is for the first two hours.

Two beat consisted of seamy broken down tenements and low class bars. Even Bill's uniform was shabby, as if trying to merge into the background. A form of camouflage, not dirty, and all the other cops down there seemed the same. By midnight my enthusiasm was waning dramatically. I'd been training hard with the weights all day and was knackered.

'Do y'mind if we had a rest Bill?'

He laughed. 'Rest? You haven't started yet, all you bloody athletes are the same, soft as shite.'

'Aye, well I've been training all day and haven't been to bed.'

'You big baby, okay, howay we'll sit in the park pavilion for ten minutes.'

'Park?' I didn't think there could possibly be such a place within miles, but up a back lane he took me to Summerhill Park. A square green oasis surrounded by Georgian buildings, alas degenerating to rack and ruin.

Despite the cold it was a clear night and the moon seemed to shine directly on us. Dew glinted on the grass as we settled into the shelter. It was more a hut with a bench, obscene graffiti all over and the acrid stench of urine cleared my sinuses. My feet were throbbing, I tipped my hat back, relaxed then involuntarily closed my eyes. The lids were heavy, I began drifting while Bill puffed contentedly on his pipe, the smell of sweet tobacco taking us into a magic moment of tranquillity.

'Just as easy to polis like this Arthur ... lay low for a little while, let the beat settle.' I could hear him in the mists, but beginning to wish I was tucked up in my warm bed. I'm sure whatever he said was very interesting, but I was fighting sleep now and forced my eyes open. Suddenly a movement on the other side of the park caught my eye. Instantly adrenaline pumped, alert as a rabbit in a cornfield when he knows a farmer has him in his sights.

'Bill,' I uttered excitedly, nearly shouting my whisper, 'There's a car with no lights. It's rolling down without its engine.' Bill looked up calmly.

'Aye you're right, might be a couple of prigs trying to twoc it ... come on.' He knocked his pipe out, and we sprinted over the damp grass diagonally, silently bat like. A crouching run, excitement coursed through my veins, a feeling I was to experience hundreds of times during my career and became totally hooked on! We dived behind a bush. I peered into the gloom.

'It's stopped. There's two guys getting out Bill. They're coming this way.' I couldn't believe our luck, my heart was thumping and body trembling. I swore I could also hear Bill's.

'Let's jump them!' I wanted to leap out that instant edging forward, but he held me back firmly.

'No, wait, right. NOW!' and we pounced like two 'leather aprons' grabbing a body each. They were rooted to the spot in fear.

'Aye so where you two guys off to?' Neither man replied. Bill indicated the parcel one of them was carrying.

'What's that?' I hadn't actually seen it in the dark, but Bill tore the corner of some newspaper wrapping away and to my amazement, in the torch light I saw the claw ends of two large jemmies sticking out. Bill grabbed his man firmly and turned to me.

'Search him Arthur, and don't take any crap.' I didn't have to be told twice and searched my prisoner who looked a real tough customer, but remained totally silent. From each of his jacket pockets I withdrew what appeared to be blocks of margarine, plus sever metal discs with wires attached. I showed them to Bill who shrugged.

'Put them in your pockets they might have done a Co-op.' He then said to both of them. 'I'm arresting you both for being in possession of house-breaking implements.' Housebreaking implements! Fantastic! The sort of case some coppers dream of, but never get a sniff in the whole of their service. I was green as grass but knew that much. Bill whispered as we walked towards the car which was parked further up the road. 'Careful, they're a couple of nasty bastards.'

I gripped mine tightly as we marched towards the motor car which alarmingly coughed into life and accelerated towards us. Purely on reflex I pushed my man into its path, and he stumbled into the headlights forcing it to stop. The driver leaned from the window beaming a smile.

'Good evening officers, can I be of assistance?' It was laughable, our prisoners glowered at him.

'Aye, do you know where the West End Police Station is?'

'Yes I do.' This was something out of the Beano. I must be dreaming or it was an elaborate wind up. Bill was so calm and collected.

'Well I'm commandeering this car. Take us there please.'

'Certainly officer.' We all climbed into the rear seat of the old Daimler and I sat between the prisoners, Bill next to the driver. My heart pounding even harder, the apprehension about two violent prisoners spinning my head. Purely in self preservation I left the doors open partially on the catch and warned them both.

'Any bother I'll push you out ... right?' It was a bluff, but they remained still and silent. Violent? I couldn't understand, if it had been me in their position I would have had a real go. The car glided through the back lanes and the driver was making small talk about the weather. What the hell was going on? Up to Elswick Road I spotted two men kicking in the front door of a shop.

'Bill there's two more.' Bill winked.

'Bird in the hand son.' The driver willing to assist, interjected.

'I'll stop if you like?'

'Get y'bloody foot down pal.' The words spat from Bill's mouth like rifle shots. Without radios or other communication we were powerless and the shop breakers had to be allowed to get away with it.

Five minutes later we entered the West End Police Station and I was instructed to sit in a back room with our prisoners after they were searched. All their property was listed including the jemmies, margarine and metal discs and wires. I honestly didn't have a clue as to what was going on. Newby Wiske procedures seemed to have flown out the window. The prisoners just dog eyed me, and Bill was right they did look a couple of mean bastards. Formalities over, they were placed in the cells and the Station Sergeant, Wyndham Thompson, came to see me with a big smile and a warm handshake.

'I'm putting you in my memoirs young McKenzie ... cracking case son ... it's a wonder you weren't all blown sky high.'

'What do you mean sergeant?'

'Y'mean you don't know?'

'I haven't a clue.'

'It's bloody dynamite son, and it's sweating. Those metal things are pigging detonators.' I broke into a sweat myself. Explosives. What a case!

'If that lot had gone up you would have taken half of the West End with you … well done son.'

The following day it hit the headlines, I'd gone from zero to seventy in one fell swoop, immediate status and news travelled the force like wildfire. It didn't stop there however, for after a sleepless day I almost ran back to the Cattle Market to start the next night. This time I was allocated to patrol with an older cop, a rough and ready cockney who resembled a rag man more than a police officer. A loner, he didn't care a fig about the system, having bucked it several years earlier, ensuring his prospects were to walk the beat the rest of his service. A solid cop but a totally different to Bill.

My first night on duty goes off with a bang.

'Wite artside mite, I'll be there in a jiff.' He was going to keep me firmly in my place … I could tell. So I dutifully paced outside the slaughter houses. The stench of putrefaction was overpowering, drifting from a huge handcart loaded up with beasts' innards. I gagged on the smell, so I turned to face down wind as my stomach began to turn. As I turned a motor cycle drew up to the junction, nothing suspicious, but I had to stick my nose in.

'Your bike lad?' He didn't answer and stared straight ahead, but the look in his eye told me he was ready for the off! Without hesitation I jumped in front of him as he revved it and I knew … I just knew it was nicked.

'Okay, where'd you pinch it?'

'Car park round the back … look I'll take it back.' Take it back? I should cocoa. I grabbed him in sheer delight and after a tussle dragged him into the section house. Old Ted, who resembled Corky the Kat looked up, well served with beer, a belligerent red faced antique copper.

'What y'got there son … a twocker?' My grin told him and the others. Ted continued, 'I think we've got a golden bollicks on our hands here lads.' He'd christened me with a classic and I was happy to be accepted by such as Ted, for they could make your life a misery. The nickname stuck with me for years (others includes Peter Pan, Indiana Jones and Big Nasty Bastard), but without that first success whose to know, if I'd got involved with a lazy womanising drunkard instead of Bill where I would have ended up … because plenty of them did!

After touring the outer divisions I returned to my permanent posting in the Central, and eager to show what I could do. Normally you would spend the first few months filling in for holidays or waiting for dead men's shoes, but to my delight I was immediately put onto a shift and given the responsibility of a patch (beat). I was always a bit of a loner and steered away from boozing or socialising too much as my driving ambition was to become an International discus thrower and shot putter. This didn't go down too well with other lads on the shift and at times it was difficult to reconcile as they couldn't understand what was driving me.

'You joined to be a polis, not throw pieces of wood about a field.' They took the 'mick' remorselessly, but instead of putting me off their goading made me strive even harder. I was also determined to show everyone what a good cop I was, so doubled my efforts on the streets.

Home life was unhappy. Mother didn't approve of Irene, but being on shift work meant I was never really at home. The atmosphere was strained, but now I was a man with a mind of my own with real responsibilities. I don't think mam ever really knew or understood exactly what my job entailed and her sheltered background brought out the strangest questions. 'Have you caught any robbers lately?' Or in between shifts she would say, 'Do they know you're not at work?' The gap between us was incalculable and it wasn't until many years later that we were to come any closer. In fact it was only months before she died, yet she still retained an innocent naiveté which was so rare and precious, something parents always dread their own children losing … and mine was certainly long gone. I was itching to get stuck in and ploughed all of my efforts into work and sport, pushing home to the back of my mind. I now had my own patch and was determined to face up to the responsibility that went with it.

* * * * * * * * * * * * * * * * * * *

'Paddling the patch and Physical Cautions'

My first 'patch' six beat straddled high risk city centre shops, offices, tenements, factories, pubs, boarding houses and good class residential property. The spine was Sandyford Road with the boundaries Haymarket, Northumberland Street, Northumberland Road, winding back through Sandyford using the railway line as a division, to Jesmond Road, then back down to the Haymarket. Always on the boil and never a dull moment. In public view I strutted with thumbs hooked in my tunic pockets and attempted to be everywhere at the same time. If it moved I stopped it. I was hungry to learn and carried out my duties with zeal.

My individual style included rather high minded ideals because I genuinely thought I had to protect the public and was eager to serve them. Honest naiveté, probably inherited from my mother, and an attitude which alienated the public more than often. I quickly learned that the masses generally accept you provided you don't interfere in their lives, but always ensure you are there to take the strain when they call. Respect? Well yes to a large degree, but a vociferous undercurrent of criminals hate law and order and everything it stands for.

As patrol officer I had to maintain a fine balancing act which could only be achieved with the will and consent of the public. Mine was an uncompromising beat with violence a constant companion, especially from two of the pubs. No quarter was given and often when I commenced nights at the police pillar in Barrass Bridge trepidation turned over in my stomach waiting for the 'Sink' to spew its customers. Drunks eager for a fight, and me standing like a wooden dolly inviting every one of them to try their luck. A young, fresh faced, oven ready cop ready for the plucking, with words of wisdom from section sergeant 'Blondie' ringing in my ear.

'You don't have to lock them all up son. Dish some physical cautions out.'

'Physical cautions sarge?'

'Aye, it's the only way you'll ever earn their respect lad.' I'd never heard that one before, but it suited my approach. The police service always has an expression to sum up any given situation succinctly. Blondie watched me like a hawk. A tall, well built good looking man with flowing blonde hair parted down the centre and a well-groomed moustache. Quiet and efficient, always popping up when least expected. Other guys on the shift reckoned he was a bastard who had to be treated with suspicion and told the tale to the bosses, but I always spoke as I found and his cool efficient impressive approach gave me confidence as a probationer.

It didn't take long to be initiated and within a month I had to take a couple of good hidings and several near misses. Nothing serious, but enough to test me out, tunic off in a back lane behind the Lamberts Leap pub and overseen by the locals. I quickly learned you had to win, because there's no way you can arrest someone who has just beaten you fair and square. I was forced to bite my lip, put it down to experience and accept it. It wasn't all one sided however and the residents soon recognised I was there to do a job and prepared to do it.

The Barrass Bridge (Sink) and Lamberts Leap (The Leap) pubs were the focal points of this community. Spit, sawdust, leaded windows and packed to capacity every night. It was ten o'clock closing then and customers were reluctant to leave at the death. Invariably there would be 'lock ins' if they could get away with it and it was cat and mouse between us. One night I saw the lights on at the Sink and looking through the spy window saw about thirty all merrily knocking pints back and playing darts and dominoes. I banged on the side door and to my amazement it was opened by Blondie who thrust a pint into my hand.

'Drink it and f... off son.' A strange situation, this was my patch, yet he was my boss. I stared into his blue eyes, pushed past him with the pint and the room went silent. Deciding discretion was the better part

Barrass Bridge – rebuilding work where the Civic Centre now stands. Why is it that visionaries' dreams become our nightmare. Where the lorry is in the background is where the police pillar stood. To the left is the tree, which still stands, where I later buried a cat.

of valour I held the pint up, knocked it back in one then said, 'In future any private parties, keep the bloody curtains closed or I'll do the lot of you,' put the glass on the bar and walked out to a round of applause. Blondie followed me out.

'I'll sign your book here,' and signed it with a smile, never referring to the incident again. The curtains were always kept closed after that with the odd bottle of milk stout often left on a window sill ... which was extremely welcome, and I had very little trouble at that pub the rest of my time on the beat. The rules of the game in the late fifties were that you had to be a part of the community and not apart from it. Corruption never entered into it and never coloured any decision I made. The bulk of the community trusted me and the amount of local information I gleaned when they knew I was 'sound' was incredible.

Four o'clock on a summers afternoon, I'm four months in and turning into an old sweat, when a helpful member of the public approached me in the grounds of St Thomas' Church. It had been very pleasant up until then watching office girls sunbathing.

'The blue light's flashing on your pillar son.' Sure enough his master's light summoned me to answer the phone. There were no pocket radios or other means of communication then, just the pillars and police boxes dotted round the town. I opened the small door and lifted the handset tentatively in case some hooligan had covered it in spittle. A common occurrence … some even managed urination to that height. Anyway it was clean as a whistle.

'Four thirty?'

'Aye, go the Alexandra Crescent son. Mrs Cox – domestic.'

'What number?'

'You'll see when you get there … neighbour's phoned in.' I had to fill all the gaps in myself. Domestics could be anything from a murder to a neighbour's cat ripping up the bluebells. Everyone wronged and yet everyone is right and adding a cop to the equation invariably complicated matters. For some inexplicable reason a blue uniform on any scene deflects violence from themselves to him.

I walked slowly to Alexandra Crescent because often these flurries half sorted themselves out prior to arrival. Not this one. A small woman of forty accompanied by a girl of thirteen hurried towards me. Obviously mother and daughter they were extremely distressed, the mother sporting a bloody lip and sobbing uncontrollably. Stone faced neighbours, arms folded watched carefully, waiting to pounce on the side of right. The mother blurted her words out spraying me with blood.

'He's going mad in there, came in drunk and batted me in the gob.' Forcing her injury under my nostrils, her breath like a rancid floor cloth.

'Okay pet, I'll try and sort it for you.' The door was firmly shut. 'How do I get in?' What remedy I was going to exact if and when I gained entry was a mystery, but I attempted to appear confident. She thrust a key at me. Training school came flooding back. Always find out who possesses the rent book otherwise you could get done for trespass.

'Who's got the rent book love?'

'It's my house, we're not married.' Terrific! I could enter with impunity. Neighbours, drifted nearer, straining to hear my pearls of wisdom, began offering their own practical advice and shrewd observations.

'Lock the bastard up!'

'Animal! Poor woman … how long's she got to put up with that?'

'Watch him mind. He's like a wild animal.' Mrs Cox was trembling, I indicated a neighbour should take her and the daughter away. Nonchalantly I placed the key in the lock and the door was so loose I could have opened it with a damp sponge.

Stepping from sun light into gloom I was temporarily blinded and a small ginger thing hurtled at me in the passage. Grabbing the front of my tunic he butted me on the side of my face which crunched and a sweet salty taste of blood hit the back of my throat. The pain! I completely lost it and we rolled about in the passage locked in combat finally bursting into the living room where thrashing, kneeing and punching maintained impetus for several minutes. It was like trying to stuff a badger into a barrel, furniture and crockery were smashed relentlessly as we continued our frantic fight. Eventually my size and sobriety subdued 'Ginger' and panting, sweating and dishevelled I dragged him into the street. I wasn't a copper now, just a victor.

The small crowd in the path shrank back and I detected a silent cheer. They were all brave now, shouting at him whilst he struggled. Impulsively, instantly, I made an arbitrary decision. I drew my truncheon, bent him over the front wall and gave him four or five whacks across the seat of his trousers. He gave one or two gasps as I administered the humiliation in front of the street, then grabbing his collar thrust him back into the house.

'Right pal, that was just a traveller's sample, next time I'll open the suitcase and you'll get the rest.' He glowered, but didn't respond.

'Thanks.' Mrs Cox smiled. I'd done her dirty work.

'You won't lock him up will you?' The apprehension in her voice told me had I decided on that course of action the outcome would have been oh so different. This was long before the days of enlightenment on wife battering and domestic abuse departments.

'No pet, but if he starts again I will.' then turned to the crowd. 'Okay the show's over … nowt to see. Get y'sels away.' Reluctantly the spectators dispersed mumbling, giving hostile stares. I can only guess they had wanted Ginger's livers out and I'd sold their Gladiatorial spectacle short. Quietly pleased I briskly walked off, and anyway it was time for bait.

I retreated to Park Terrace Section House on the A1 at the corner of Exhibition Park. It comprised of two bare rooms. One had a large formica-topped table, worn over the years with years of card and domino schools, and a single bar electric fire mounted on the wall, with sink, cooker and drainer at one side. Alone, I made sure all the doors were closed and that the telephone was off the hook as I tucked myself into the other room at the rear to eat my bait. It was necessary to take such precautions otherwise you'd be inundated with calls and passers-by reporting accidents and lost dogs.

I brewed up and began reliving the situation pensively sucking at the pint pot of tea. Doubts began to peep around the corners. Christ! What had I done? I must have been crackers whacking the guy and in full view of at least a dozen witnesses. What if he complained? Bloody hell, suddenly my mouth filled with sandwich, unable to masticate it properly, the saliva refused to come. From that small whisper these thoughts turned into loud shouts. I threw the rest of my bait into the

Athlete of distinction … policeman of integrity … writer gifted with rare insight … but more importantly one of the good guys. Knowing and having Arthur as a friend is one of the most positive experiences of my life. As conventional retirement will never be part of the McKenzie understanding I'm sure there's even more to come in the years ahead. I eagerly await the next instalment.

Steve Black

bin, jammed my hat on and hurried out.

It was imperative to have an easy mind. I would have to return to the house and test the temperature. Impulsion, plus butterflies the size of rats in my stomach, five minutes later I knocked on Cox's front door and cleared my throat. It was opened by Ginger who stepped back in surprise. For what seemed an age we stared at each other, then to my amazement he gave a slow smile. He was sober now.

'You'd better come in son, we've just been talking about you.' I entered slowly, cautiously, removed my cap and was led into the living room. 'Sit down lad, sit down.' Mrs Cox was crouched over the fire, Scrooge like, a charred piece of toast lay on the arm of the chair, black as the ace of spades, fork still threaded through it.

'Bottle of Broon do y?'

'What? Eh? ... er Aye.' I was caught on the hop, he appeared a completely different person, almost human. He unhinged a bottle of lunatics broth and handed it to me. An hour earlier and it have been broken over my head with relish.

'Private pet, him and me have to talk.' She smiled and left, but I could see there wasn't a fleck of fear in her eyes. There was no sign of the daughter. He extended his hairy, horny hand.

'Put it there lad.' I took the bone crunching handshake and held it firmly.

'That's the first time anybody has knacked me. I take my hat off to you.' I was flabbergasted.

'No hard feelings eh son?'

'No ... na but you shouldn't be hitting a woman should you?' I was more relieved than he was if the truth be told. He pulled his shirt open and revealed a large bruise on his chest.

'You know what she did that with son? A flat iron, was I supposed to let her stove my head in?' The story wasn't as straight forward as first thought and I was glad I hadn't really opened the can of worms properly.

'Right then, that's the book shut ... finished. Okay son?'

'Aye, but I don't want to be called back for anything like again.'

'You've my word.' I relaxed, we chatted and I enjoyed the beer.

Ginger turned out to be an excellent contact over the next few months. My first 'snout', in the vernacular, putting several cases my way. A long distance lorry driver, he knew all the fiddles – stolen tarpaulins, batteries and such like, and had several scores to settle. Daft stuff really, but it set me out to learn the finer points of thief catching, interviewing them and getting them convicted. It horrifies me to think what I did, for any other result could have been catastrophic and the end of my career. Fortunately that was the mood of the era, of which I caught the tail end, and without doubt that particular set of circumstances became a landmark for me and possibly that family.

MUSCLES AND PUFF NUT!

Manchester Belle Vue Stadium in 1960 and the first time I won the British Police Discus Title.

No matter how hard I tried to remain an individual, attitudes within the job rubbed off, some subliminally, others overtly. Influences for good or bad constantly bombarded me from workmates. Ken Richardson, a police legend, affectionately known as 'Muscles' was such a man for the good. Motivator extraordinary, friend, but best described as a dynamic rhinoceros with the energy and drive of a nuclear reactor. Abounding with life, it was a delight to be in his presence. Eyes sharp as an eagle, reactions to match and always three steps ahead of his prey. For thirty years he carried many men to glory on his broad shoulders, yet retired as a constable, satisfied and contented. A truly happy man.

Initially I met Ken as a cadet in 1957 and we were drawn together through sport. As a tenacious prop forward with Gosforth RFC he was an England trialist, but also dabbled in shot, discus and hammer. Police District champion no less. Unusual events for unusual specimens.

'Howay puff nut, I'll show you how men do it.' I couldn't pass on such an invitation and one balmy summer evening we met in the police station yard. Nut brown Ken exuded enthusiasm as he cast the gauntlet.

'You're getting too old.' My cheeky reply slid out without thinking, and bear-like he playfully cuffed the side of the face. It hurt, and I grimaced, but made it appear as a smile.

'Cheeky sprog, come on we'll go to Fenham Barracks field for a throw, and just see whose the best eh?'

'Right, you're on.' Discovering a training partner for throwing events was almost a miracle, so changing in the station we put on plimsolls and shorts and drove in his brand new Triumph Mayflower three miles west to a field directly opposite Fenham Barracks. Empty except for a few curious children watching our heaving and straining with the 16lb hammer. A dangerous, exciting, but spectacular event and the gaggle of youngsters were joined by a man in a gas board uniform and cap.

His smile of appreciation seemed friendly enough as this honest working man leaned against the cross bar of his cycle watching our wood nymph twirls in tight shorts. I threw the hammer, Ken, spotting in the outfield, called me over.

'That dirty bugger's waving his daisy,' he said, fuming from the corner of his mouth, bushy eyebrows twitching. I glanced back and sure enough daisy waving was no exaggeration, my own temper welled up.

'I'll soon wipe the smile of the dirty bastard's face!' and in Herculean fashion swung the hammer round his head and hurled it at the flasher, missing his head by a whisker. Had it connected our man would have been exposed in some far better place. I've never seen anything move so fast in my life. Leaping onto his bike he swept from the entrance as if jet propelled. I shouted involuntarily as, to my horror, saw a trolley bus bearing down upon him. Incredibly he seemed to bend around the front of the trolley and headed off demented down Barrack Road towards the City.

Ken and I chased in hot pursuit. I ran, while Ken stood in the centre of the road and, in best pointsman style, stopped a bus travelling in the right direction. The gas man cycled furiously into the forecourt of a Suttons Dwellings where I lost him temporarily. Coming towards me wheeling a pram was a wide eyed housewife.

'Have you seen anybody come in here on a bike pet?' I panted. She looked, then pointed to her left where my man cowered in a corner.

'Got y' y'dirty swine.' My words seemed to throw an electric current through his body. In one movement he cast the cycle over an eight foot wall then scrambled after it. I turned back and ran into Barrack Road only to see his tail disappearing rapidly into the distance. Taking a deep breath I set off at a gallop, and coming towards me were three young children pushing a small cycle. Without thinking I snatched it from them and jumped on despite the fact it was three sizes too small. Total disaster! The chain snapped plummeting me head over heels into the road. Ken passed by hanging from the back of a bus screaming like a

I spy Gas Board Flashers.

banshee, 'I'll catch him mucker.'

Eventually we both ended up at the foot of Gallowgate, one and a half miles away. We'd lost our prey, my lungs were red hot and the City teeming with workers homeward bound, and there was I still dragging this tiny cycle.

'Excuse me, have you seen a bloke on a bike wearing a gas man's uniform?' My question to the pin striped office workers drew only blank looks and wry smiles. Joe public probably thought we'd escaped from some naturist institution. Dejected, we trudged wearily back to the field, a lonely sweaty journey, and an ironic indicator as to what lay ahead.

'Not to worry mucker … you win some and lose some.' Ken patted my shoulder and gave his infectious toothy grin.

Characters such as Ken come along once in a hundred life times. His extrovert personality hid a discerning mind capable of a rationale way ahead of adversaries, who would often pick and snipe behind his back. Clearly they were jealous of his success which was truly spectacular. To me it appeared the whole City revolved around him and who he didn't know wasn't worth knowing – either side of the fence. Ken worked our relief, but on another beat and whilst we did bump into each other the constrictive beat system meant it was only occasionally. Examining the future work details I noticed I had been marked to work with Ken on the general purposes (G.P.) crime car the following nightshift and I couldn't wait for it to arrive. G.P. duty was a jealously guarded plum, using an unmarked police car on a roving commission to catch criminals. The phone rang, it was Muscles.

'Out with me next week eh mucker?'

'Aye Ken.'

'Right, get in about nine, we'll round a few drunks up before we start to get us in the mood eh mucker?'

'You bet.' Even on the telephone his contagious motivation permeated down the wires.

First night of G.P. I walked into the charge room about quarter to nine with trepidation, for Ken's reputation for becoming involved in physical combat was well documented. My own altercations paled into insignificance by comparison. I pushed the doors to the charge room open and Ken was waiting, impish grin across his cheeky face, shouting in boyish delight.

'You're too late mucker, I've two in already.' Sweeping his arms aside to display two drunken louts being processed at the charge desk.

'Right, get your civvie jacket on.' There was no time for thoughts as we breezed into the yard. It was like a dream, because this was what I'd imagined the job was all about. Ken's driving was like his personality – wild and immediate and we zipped out the archway into Pilgrim Street.

'Haymarket – Right?'

'Anywhere you like.' I hadn't a clue, but he seemed to know what he was doing and we screamed up Northumberland Street into the Haymarket. He covered so much ground it took my breath away. The

Haymarket was quiet except for a solitary motorist bending over the boot of his car outside a cafe. Ken's antennae were out.

'What's he doing?' He seemed perfectly innocent to me.

'Evening sir.' Ken screamed to a halt and shouted from the window.

'Yes?' The man appeared dazed, 'What's the matter?'

'Your car?' Ken was out, examining every aspect of the vehicle.

'Do you know your tyre is flat at the front?'

'Er … no,' and he walked round to examine it puzzled. Immediately Ken grabbed his arm like a striking cobra.

'Right, what's that you were loading into the boot?' I was taken aback, uncertain, what the hell was Ken up to?

'What do you mean? I've done nothing wrong.' The man's eyes and voice amplified his fear.

'Mucker, get a clock.' I peered into the boot and pulled a sheet aside to reveal a large tray of chocolate eclairs.

'Cakes Ken – tray full.'

'Right mister, what about it before I check this out properly?' Not menacing, just direct, his nose was telling him and the response unbelievable.

'Okay, I've just taken them from this cafe. I'm the cook.' Ken gave a triumphant victory guffaw.

'First one in the bag mucker.' The poor unfortunate cook was whisked to the station, processed and placed in the cells. It was nine fifteen.

'Right let's get another.' Sergeant Alec Cameron interrupted.

'Get this one sorted first or you'll have the cells full.'

'With respect sergeant.' Ken tugged my sleeve and we left. The sergeant had no control whatsoever, Ken's personality was too strong and I was being carried along on the tide.

We quickly visited the Haymarket cafe to check out statements and then zoom! Down Percy Street through the traffic lights at the junction with Blackett Street.

'Ken you jumped a red.'

'Ginger mucker, they were on ginger,' and laughed.

'Ah, what's that I see?' and jammed the brakes on, tyres squealing.

'Grab him!' and pointed to a man staggering up the street carrying an eight foot sack of peas. Punch drunk I jumped from the car and stopped him. Ken joined us laughing and waving the man towards the car in a 'Raleigh' bow and sweeping motion said, 'Will you kindly step into the car please sir?'

'But I bought them from a man in a pub Ken.' He roared with laughter and obviously knew the punter well.

Arresting him and squeezing the sack in the car was a sight to behold, but by half past nine we were back in the charge room with the enormous sack of peas on the floor. Ken was in his element, but I could see paper work coming to meet us by the ton.

'Ken, do you not think we should sort this lot out before we get some more?' He playfully punched me in the stomach temporarily winding me.

Newcastle City Police Rugby XV in 1957. I am on the back row on the right. Muscles is front row seated 3rd from left – with a real 'mucker' look on his face.

Muscles – inspirational in every sense of the word and truly the 'man for the moment'. Here he is behind me making sure I don't step out of line. (I make no comment for the fact that it's the only time I saw him with a pen in his hand.)

'They've warned you about me haven't they?'

'No.' I was embarrassed, my lie showed. Why lie to a guy like this?

'Well aye, they did say you had an aversion to paper work.'

'Paper work's easy chuffnut ... it's burglars that are hard. Come on, let's get out and stuck into them.' I didn't need telling twice, so out we went.

Change of tack this time, up Northumberland Street and along Ellison Place, a good sneck for catching car thieves or suspected persons. The car park was empty, but Ken spotted a shadow against the wall opposite the YWCA and he skidded the motor onto the ash car park and had the punter right in the headlights. We got out and walked towards him, Ken whispered, 'He's got two pairs of pants on.' How he knew was beyond me. Anyway, sure enough when we searched him in the rear pocket of the second pair of jeans was a cheque stub, and he couldn't tell us whose name was on it. It transpired he had done a string of house burglaries in Gosforth on the North Road and the cheque book had come from one of them. A terrific case or 'chalk' as they were called, and it turned out the punter was wanted all over the country for similar offences. As Gosforth was then in the separate force of Northumberland we handed him over and it was only half past ten. The whole shift lay ahead of us.

Patrolling with Ken in the warmth of the car was luxury compared to the streets, but more appealing was the atmosphere. He encapsulated in both words and actions everything I had been searching for. There was no way I could copy him, but his attitude and approach was infectious. If I could somehow tap into that I knew I could use it as a tool. As the night wore on no opportunity was allowed to pass, we stopped everybody and everything. When at 4 am he once again jerked the car to a halt I naturally thought the tramp reclining in the shop doorway at the top of Northumberland Street was on his way to a police cell.

'Hang fire kidda.' Ken sauntered over to the vagrant and began chatting, then to my complete surprise gave him some money and returned. This was a side to Muscles character very few had observed.

'Did you give that tramp money?' He grabbed me by the tunic front. 'He's a human being mucker, just hope that it isn't you one day, and if it is hope somebody like me comes along and gives you two half crowns.' I went quiet, suitably rebuked, having never thought along those lines before. He'd hit me right to the core and for a few minutes there was an uncanny silence in the car as I regained composure.

Up to then I had treated vagrants with disdain, for a veritable army of such destitutes plagued six beat. Sleeping rough they infested everything with vermin and I never ever considered doing them any favours. The following night back on the beat after my crash course on the G.P. car I set about duty with a new fervour and Ken's words were about to echo in my ears. The patch had suffered a high incidence of milk thefts from doorsteps and I strongly suspected tramps. It didn't take half a brain to detect this, for half of the houses were being demolished to make way for 'progress' and in the interim period these properties provided community accommodation for scavengers. To be honest, I liked scavenging myself and found a mass disposal ground of rancid milk bottles at the rear an old deserted house adjacent to Sandyford railway station.

Determined to catch the culprits, I crept into the yard of this house and could hear noises coming from the coal house. Gathering myself I yanked the door open and shone my torch into the inky darkness and certainly didn't expect the sight which greeted my innocent blue eyes. Two well known 'knights' of the road nicknamed 'Omo and Daz' were performing an act which can only be described as repulsive. Riveted to the spot I was at a loss to know how to arrest these partially clothed, lice infested bodies. Without going into the gory details I managed to shepherd them to the police station much to the alarm and dismay of Fergie the station sergeant.

'Okay kidda, you arrested them, so you search them.' The stench was indescribable and the soggy contents of their pockets withdrawn. Everything from rolled up newspapers, old crusts of bread, handfuls of cigarette ends – I nearly vomited. The police surgeon's examination was even more gruesome, but Fergie quietly stood relishing my discomfort, and ensured I remained in close contact with my prisoners. Ever since our first encounter he kept me under such pressure in what can only be described as a sadistic way.

Finally the tramps were charged with gross indecency and I almost ran to the RVI for injections, then burned my uniform at the first opportunity. Not a pleasant experience, but my actions had the desired effect and all milk thefts stopped. Both men pleaded guilty and sentenced to prison, but the biggest impact was from poor old 'Daz' who died in prison. I vividly recall the last occasion he was being placed in the prison van. Looking at me with dark sunken, pain ridden eyes, he spoke directly into my soul.

'Don't look at me like that son, remember we're all somebody's babies.' It made me shiver, it still does. Muscles was absolutely right!

* * * * * * * * * * * * * * * * * * *

'I'm not afraid of dying, I just don't want to be there when it happens.' – Woody Allen

Death has by far the biggest impact on the job. It hits you between the eyes and begs every unanswerable question. My introduction to its finality was stark, macabre and something leeched from a horror film only weeks into my service.

Refreshment breaks at Park Terrace meant heavy card schools. The old stagers loved their three card brag, blinding every hand and taking young lads like myself to the cleaners. Strangely enough sitting with them in that situation brought out their real personalities, tempers frayed and singularity of purpose always prevailed. Sometimes if the sergeant wasn't around and the inspector had gone off duty these would last all night.

On this day in question big 'Stewy' walked in carrying a large crisp tin. 'Deal us in man,' and sat muffled at one end of the formica topped table, pushed his hat to the back of his head and put the crisp tin firmly on a chair beside him.

'Big bait tonight Stewy?' I attempted a funny. He said nothing, smiled grimly, prised the lid from the tin with his nails and pulled out a female human head, gory and torn. Shock! I nearly fainted, but the others never flinched. George looked up from his cards and in a matter of fact tone said, 'Put it back man, she can see my hand,' and while the laughs removed the immediate sting my mind was in a turmoil at this unbelievable situation. I couldn't help thinking the poor woman had washed her face and combed her hair that morning. The head had come from a multiple fatal accident at the Blue House traffic lights a mile up the road. The bodies had been whisked off to the RVI, but the head was found in the garden of the Blue House later. En route to the hospital with it Stew hadn't wanted to miss his card game!

Coping with other people's grief is always traumatic, very little can actually be done except to remain as tender and sympathetic as possible. Dealing with death on a daily basis there is always the danger of becoming cynical, but in the quiet moments this veneer disappears and realisation dawns that no one is immune. This finality constantly followed me and I never could get used to it.

I vividly remember my first 'stiff'. A hot summer's Sunday morning about nine o'clock. I was standing at Eldon Square police box on Blackett Street and the blue flasher went.

'430?'

'Go to the Green Market son, somebody there has a story to tell.'

'Right.' My guts told me what it was and I walked with dread to the Green Market in Clayton Street. In those days there were flats above the market, dirty dingy, smelly places overrun with rats and wild cats. An old couple anxiously waited for me outside a peeling brown door. Pale and strained they held on to each other for physical and moral support.

'Upstairs,' says he.

'What is it?' They both looked as if the grim reaper had them within arms length as well.

'We haven't seen her for three months and the radio's playing.'

'Why have you waited so long to tell us?'

'We thought she'd gone to her daughter's down South. Didn't want to interfere.' Climbing the rackety staircase I could smell it on the way up. There's never any mistake, the stench of death lingers in the nostrils and permeates everywhere. The neighbours followed hesitantly, and I knew what was expected of me, but the urge to turn and run was more than real.

'Get the kettle on, there's a love. I'll be in to see you in a minute.' Both shuffled into their flat directly opposite glancing at the door. A door leading to a corpse, we all knew that. Sure enough I could hear the wireless playing but there was also a loud hissing noise. The neighbours closed their door, I waited a few seconds to gather myself, then boot up, smash! The door shattered and the top hinge became

The Old Green Market. This must have been taken on a Sunday morning. A busy, exciting place to patrol, with smells of fruit and vegetables, fish and diesel oil with the banter and oaths of the waggon drivers as they attempted to off-load. The cop in charge – affectionately known as 'Snotty O'Brien' – a large man with ferocious eyes and Florentine face – would bark them into total confusion. But the job got done.

detached. Immediately I reeled, not so much from the smell, but the sheer volume of bluebottles which hit me like a cloud of locusts. I retched, good job I hadn't had a big breakfast, then wrapping my tie round my mouth and nose rushed in and smashed the windows by punching them out through closed curtains, releasing the putrefied air. Bluebottles everywhere I was forced to retreat. Two pairs of watery frightened eyes were peeping from behind their door. I pushed and entered. She had brewed up, best china out, and her hand shook as she poured the tea. I had to give the room time to settle.

'Is she dead?' I nodded gently and tried to remain calm.

'Oh my God, it'll be us next.' She began crying and trembling.

'Come on pet.' That's all I could say and put my arm round her frail shoulders. I couldn't think of anything else other than I could have a prile of them at this rate.

'Have you a towel?' He looked. 'I need to go back in.' The old man pulled out what must have been their best towel and I wrapped it round my face for protection. Clasping it tightly I re-entered the small room which was no more than twelve by ten. In the centre stood a large table upon which there were lumps of bread, bottles and a casserole dish alive with maggots. The room was coming in on me and messy, an old gas stove, a pile of coal and several buckets containing excreta. I searched, no sign of the body, nothing in the bed and in frustration I even searched a chest of drawers and picked up a few lumps of coal. Stumped, I was forced to contact the station for assistance.

Derek Carter an older, wiser colleague arrived speedily, and brought his experience to bear. Pulling the sheets off the bed he pointed to maggots squirming through the mattress, then hoisting it up revealed a pitiful bundle lying between it and the springs where she had crawled for warmth. The situation became even more gory when the police surgeon arrived and I had to assist in straightening the body by standing on the arms and legs. Not a pleasant experience, but something I had to live through on many other occasions.

That set the ball rolling, I went through a spell in those first two years, but one in particular really knocked me for six. My first Christmas on the beat and I thought I couldn't become emotionally involved. How wrong I was. The biggest drawback in working Christmas is having to watch everyone enjoying themselves whilst you wrestle with their problems. Christmas day 1959, night shift and, only two of us covering Jesmond, a huge area. It was a sharp frosty evening, treacherous under foot and a slight dusting of snow over black ice. Tinsel, fairy lights and decorations winked from windows and now and again the silence was broken by a burst of spontaneous merry making. That depressed me and by quarter past eleven the night was bitterly cold and cheerless. Walking slowly along Highbury ahead of me an old gent was attempting to negotiate the incline over the railway lines heading towards Osborne Road. He was well muffled against the elements, and I could see his maroon scarf and string backed gloves in the lamp light. In dismay I noticed his galoshes, and immediately knew he shouldn't be wearing them. The words had hardly entered my mind when he staggered and slipped. His head hit the ground with a sickening bong! Cap flying. I ran forward, but there was nothing I could do. He was dead.

A terrible feeling of guilt overcame me as I put my hands into his pockets for I could still feel his body warmth, yet no life. His spectacles case contained a name and address and it's amazing how many old people still do that. It could have been my dad. A passing motorist stopped and an ambulance arrived. It was down to me to inform the relatives, a difficult task at the best of times, but Christmas? The address was only a couple of streets away and minutes later I knocked and waited. Celebrations were going on inside and an attractive, smiling young woman came to the door.

'Happy Xmas ossifer,' she giggled, 'Have I been naughty and parked my car without lights?' and giggled again. I took my cap off and looked past her into the passage, a man holding a glass of beer was walking towards the door.

'I better come in love.'

'Yes, what is it? Come in come in.' The look in my eye told her. She collapsed. How do you tell a daughter that her father, who was earlier enjoying his meal and still has unopened Christmas presents in his pockets is now lying dead in the hospital morgue? Her husband, zombie like, placed his glass on the stairs and put his arms round his wife. There was nothing I could say and left quickly, for to intrude on private grief seemed an obscenity. Outside the street was the same, lights still twinkling, with pockets of merrymakers bidding farewells. I felt so angry I wanted to harangue them, they had no right to be happy when an old man had just died.

I often reflected on that incident about my thoughts prior to the old man slipping. Had they occurred before or after the event? A trick of the mind? Whatever it was, I shared his last seconds on this earth and was powerless to change fate.

'Inform' messages or 'deathograms' as they are sometimes called become routine police work, but to knock on any door usually spells heartache for the recipient, but not always. The Haymarket was alive with paper sellers, each rattling and rustling red hot news. One such man, a Jack the lad who had pulled himself up by his boot straps through petty crime, fiddles, ducking and diving was proud of his paper patch. One dinner time I had to inform him of his father's death and this is how the conversation went.

'Hello Mac, all right son?'

'It's a bit sensitive. About your dad.'

'Aye, what about the old bastard?'

'Bad news I'm afraid.'

'Dead is he?'

'Yea, I'm sorry.'

'Sorry? I'm pleased. I hope he rots in hell.' All the while continuing to shout and sell newspapers.

'But it's your dad.' I was becoming irritated. He faced me up.

'Hey, look at me, what do you see? I'll tell you what I am. A thief! That bastard brought me up to be a thief! No, I owe him nowt and I want nowt to do with it.'

'You mean you're not even going to go and see him?'

'I've told you, no and the Corporation can bury him – the bastard!' and walked away. I couldn't believe what had happened, but it made me realise that life is complex, but death has the biggest impact – it is without equal.

SECTION SIX

BATTER, BURGLARS AND A BOMBAY SWEAT

Here I am outside Park Terrace Section House on the corner of Exhibition Park. Sadly, another police refuge gone to dust. In 25 years time some whizz-kid in architectural reclamation will decide to rebuild these section houses in an effort to encourage community policing.

Long before the days of 'carry outs' the fish shop was the centre of the universe on Sandyford Road – a steamy, thriving gastronomic refuge. When the pubs cascaded out it was as if the proprietor had thrown a magnet, drawing the whole neighbourhood into its fishy web. Most altercations involved queue jumpers, but rarely any serious problems and rendered down to good natured banter with the batter. I always tried to make it a port of call around eleven to sweep out stragglers, but one night fortunately I arrived half and hour early. I could hear the screams fifty yards away and on arrival had to force my way through the melée. Inside, a group of angry customers were holding a young Ghanian above the fish fryer, intent on dumping him into it. His screams were accompanied by a bucking twisting, kicking panic!

'How.' I shouted at the top of my voice. 'What the f ... do you think you bastards are doing?' The crowd went silent, the Ghanian still dangling precariously. 'Are you lunatics or what?' The heat was intense.

A voice shouted, 'Black bastard, jumping the bloody queue.' The reality of the language was even stronger and more venomous than this and upon reflection gives only a hint of the flavour of the times. The Ghaniain began squealing, they released him and he went into verbal overdrive, berating me.

'I want my supper. This is racial discrimination man.' I couldn't believe it and the crowd turned ugly again.

'See, the arrogant bastard, you should have let us fry him.' and they meant business. The Ghanian was screaming about rights and democracy, and began pushing me. This was one of the most inflammatory situations I had encountered so I forcibly pulled him through the crowd into the street as kicks and punches were aimed at both of us. I dragged him well away and told him in no uncertain terms if he didn't go home quietly I would arrest him because he was drunk. He attempted to punch my face shouting, 'You are low caste, I am chief, get out of my way I'm going for my supper.' There was no alternative, I arrested him, much to the delight of the cheering mob. Once restrained he began pleading about deportation and having his allowances cut, but once the grip was on I had been taught never to let go and managed to drag, persuade, and cajole him to Market Street where he was officially incarcerated. Returning to the fish shop the manager told me trouble had flared when the Ghanian had attempted to ride his motor scooter into the shop. 'Motor scooter?' This was a brand new equation, 'where is it now?' He shrugged, so I went outside, and found an NSU Quickly smashed to pieces and dumped in a front garden. The mob had taken their retribution and given a message, not only to my prisoner, but to me.

I never felt the same about the fish shop after that, but still called regularly for my bag of scratchings which I consumed in a back lane opposite. The following night, clasping my greasy newspaper wrap, I was leaning against the Dundas Garage wall devouring my meal when suddenly the hair on my neck bristled. As I peered into the night, I nearly jumped out of my skin, for there dangling from the gutter at shoulder height was a pair of legs. I grabbed, tugged and deposited the rest of my fish and chips into his face and a soft bubbling noise emitted from him. Yes, he had filled his trousers, commonly known as a 'Bombay sweat' in the business. Incredibly this burglar was on the garage roof after screwing it and about to leave as I'd turned the corner. He must have hung there for a couple of minutes poor bugger. The chips in the face are easy to explain. Harry, a marvellous old copper, once helped me in searching a warehouse on the Quayside. Eventually we found the intruder hiding in a cardboard box and immediately Harry gave him one in the stomach.

'What was that for Harry?' I asked him later.

'Always establish who's the boss mister. He'd have done the same to me given half a chance. In panic, some guys you catch will kill you so there's no way I'm going to be on a post mortem slab in the morning. Always look after number one son.' Extreme, but understandable. Harry belonged to real old school and put me right on many occasions.

'Stop chewing gum kidda. Everybody looks at a copper kidda. If you walked up the Bigg Market with no kecks on they'd all follow like sheep. So stop chewing.' I did as he said, there was no need for a sergeant when Harry was around.

The Bigg Market Newcastle – many is the drunk I have chased round the drinking fountain. My house, the Tardis, is on the left. I smashed my 'stick' (truncheon) on the old Town Hall wall to the right – throwing it at a wanted man making good his escape in a Vauxhall Victor. I never did catch him. But I've still got the stick.

Dipping into those first two years it is difficult to impart just how electric and exciting they were. Every day was a learning experience and I would talk to anyone and everyone, the older the better. Bill, the night watchie in Sandyford Road was by far my favourite. What a character, and in full control of his corrugated metal hut. These were marvellous refuges, affording warmth, company and on some occasions sleep. I would visit Bill about three times during the course of a shift. He was the eyes and ears of the street. A small, rotund, dirty, rancid individual, he behaved uncivilly to everyone, with language to match. His heavy jowled, unshaven face would emerge from the bowels of the cabin and all that could be seen were two protruding red, watery eyes. Some years earlier he'd suffered a heart attack, yet he still worked long unsociable and difficult hours. I often shared his bottle of beer or a mug of tar-like tea.

I liked him because he behaved completely naturally, no affectation, never stepping out of character, yet there was a touch of evil. Many nights I spent inhaling carbon monoxide fumes as they wafted into the cabin. Eyes heavy, head nodding, I would hear his voice droning in the distance as he put the world to right.

'Hey son … hey! Watch this.' I shuddered from my doze. His face was two inches from mine. He pushed his sweaty body past me and pointed to the corner of the cabin. 'I'll teach them.'

'Who?'

'Look and learn,' and gave a red gummed grin. I peered into the back and attempted to focus. Then I saw it. A rat! A big brown, long tail creeping through a hole at the rear.

'Christ!'

'Sshhh!' and we watched as the rodent began chewing the lump of sandwich he had judiciously placed there. Slowly Bill slipped his hand into his top pocket and withdrew a dart. Then with the speed of light threw it, catching the rat in the neck. It ran squealing round the cabin, chased by Bill who trapped it and finished it off with a large shovel. Splat! Puffing and panting I vividly remember his yellow teeth shining in the fire glow as he lifted it by the tail and threw it onto the brazier. The carcass sizzled after an initial puff of flame, and a strong smell of singeing fur wafted in. Wiping the blood from the dart onto his boiler suit and holding the shovel aloft like a gladiator he uttered some real Geordie words of wisdom.

'This is the shovel the Irish navvies use to cook their breakfasts on. That'll teach them to come over here for six months and fiddle the tax,' and began laughing uncontrollably. He was obviously mad! Sadly, a few weeks later, he was found dead in his cabin and I have to admit I missed him, but not half as much as the six beat rodent population!

* * * * * * * * * * * * * * * * * *

It's not what you know, but who you know

Marriage plans to Irene were well advanced and the final break with my parents came when I arrived home one afternoon to find my personal effects lying in the front garden. Upsetting to say the least, but what really hurt was she had torn up all photographs of me as a child underlining the turmoil which must have been going through her mind. A damp basement flat in Akenside Terrace, Jesmond became my home. We'd bought some furniture, so until our wedding in July 1960 I lived on my own. It was no big deal because shifts, work load and training kept me well occupied.

My final two year probationary report was looming and this would determine whether my services as a cop were to be retained. With four commendations for outstanding police work and having worked like a dog I was confident my future was secure until approached by George Hawksby my new section sergeant.

'Mac, a word son?' A quiet soul, George wouldn't do anyone a bad turn. Embarrassment was written all over his face.

'Yes sarge?'

'I've just seen your section sergeant's report and he's recommending your services be terminated.' The words cut like a knife through my soul. I'd had a change of supervision in recent weeks and this news was drastic. I felt sick, marriage commitments, never mind the disgrace.

'What have I done?'

'He sees you as a threat to the public.'

'A what? A threat to the bloody public. So what have I been doing these past months, sticking my neck out for them?' George smiled wryly.

'Mac, you've a lot to learn son. It's not what you do in this job, but who you know. I haven't long to do, but you've got the rest of your life. The job's in decline, no backbone and I'll be damned if I'll let them give you the push. You're a natural as far as I'm concerned so I'm seeing the inspector.'

The wind was knocked out of my sails. The police force is no different from any other organisation. It is riddled with petty-fogging, small minded people, jealousy and back stabbing is just as much a part of it as the comradeship, but fortunately there were men like George, salt of the earth who had a sense of right and wrong. Good as his word, a day later I was sent for by shift inspector Joe Scott. Heavy faced, dark skinned, never a smile, he looked as if he needed a good ironing. A disciplinarian with ability to put the fear of God into you just by a look. Strength of character oozed from him and until that meeting I'd hated his guts. I entered his office, stomach churning.

'Walk positive man. I'm not going to chop your balls off?'

'No sir.'

'Right, sit down damn you, you're blocking the light.' I did his bidding and somehow felt more at ease for there was humour in his tone.

'This bloody report of yours. What the hell have you been doing upsetting the sergeants?'

'I can't understand it sir ... all I've been doing is trying my best.'

'Look lad,' he leaned forward and pointed. 'I was in the army with your father.' I was astounded. I hadn't known.

'A fine man. Goodness knows where you came from,' then laughed loudly and continued.

'Don't ever change lad. You're coppering right! Trouble is, if you do, you'll always stand on somebody's toes. The league of frightened men!

Remember this son, always keep the eyes in your arse open, because if you don't they'll be on you like pack rats. Pack rats! Do you hear me?'

'I do sir yes, but it's never been pointed out that I'd been doing anything wrong.'

'You're working lad, that's what's wrong. Causing problems, putting them in a position where they have to make decisions!' He paused, gave me a long stare and time for his words to sink in.

'Right, I'm changing your report. If I can't help the son of an army colleague I can't help anybody. Those bastards up there are feathering their nests and turning into chocolate backed generals. Right lad, get out there and keep locking them up – understand?' He pointed out of the window into Market Street.

'Right sir.'

'Right lad – that's it.' The interview was terminated and I never saw him again, but I never forgot him or George Hawksby for what they did.

Having squeezed through the net I was now being allowed to fly and that was an extremely comfortable feeling. My service was only just commencing and that which had gone before was only tentative steps on the jungle fringes. Once through probation pressure is effectively removed, no need to do anything other than that which you have to. Some colleagues unconsciously sat back at that stage to await retirement, but that was never my philosophy. I wanted every second of excitement and went out of my way to complicate life by becoming involved. If it smelled wrong I looked into it, poked and pried until I had uncovered a nerve, using each new experience as a building block. My ambition was to catch criminals. I didn't crave to be in CID, just to catch prigs on the patch. Contrary to public perception CID did not catch the majority of criminals, the beat man usually did the initial capture and CID followed up. Obviously murders and major crime were dealt with exclusively by CID, but very often it was the beat man and his knowledge of the streets which led to successful conclusions even in those cases. Any police officer who wants to catch criminals must desire it badly and understand how to go about it. It requires hard work, dedication, luck and snouts. Get them all together and you've got success. With this philosophy I set about my task.

* * * * * * * * * * * * * * * * * * * *

Religion, promotion and secret societies – a reality check

I was moved onto eleven beat at the other end of town. Not as big, but just as interesting. The boundaries were Newgate Street, past the Co-op, right along Clayton Street West to Westgate Road, then up Bath Lane and right past West Walls. Compact and tight with trouble. I teamed up with a true father figure and mentor, Brian Hardie, who worked the adjacent beat. We hit it off instantly. Well on in service, he carried medal ribbons of honour from the war and his impact on my career was probably the most valuable. Outwardly quiet with a soft voice, he forced you to listen in order that you heard his words. Tall, with thinning sandy hair and a face covered in freckles, the ultimate in cynicism with a sense of humour second to none. Despite his appearance he was physically and mentally lethal.

'Right kid, check all your heavy property, banks, pubs and that and I'll see you about half past eleven.' Words slid from the corner of his mouth. He certainly kept a weathered eye on me ensuring I checked all my property. Again, no sergeant required.

He pointed out all the tea spots and snecks and it was surprising how many holes and corners could be found on a damp night. Brian inculcated in me the fundamentals of the job and we would have long talks. Early one morning as we were standing under the Goldsmith's clock in Grainger Street putting the world to right, I was extolling fears of the Cuban missile crisis when Brian looked round casually as if not wanting to be overheard.

'It's not the bomb you want to worry about kid. We've got a race problem in this country and if we don't learn to live in peace with each other – it could destroy the world.' I was appalled because it was a view I had never considered and was angry to think my friend might be a bigoted racist. It wasn't until later, and Enoch Powell's 'Rivers of Blood' speech, that I realised what he was trying to tell me, and how philosophical Brian was. Whenever I see the Goldsmith's clock I remember that conversation.

He also opened my mind up to other matters.

'Are you in the craft kid?' I didn't know what he was talking about.

'You'll have to join the square son.'

'What the hell are you on about Brian?'

'The masons man. Never heard of them?' Of course I had, I'd seen their golf tournaments printed on the back page of the Chronicle, but didn't understand what it was all about. Brian chuckled.

'Never wondered why they all fight to get onto the one shift?' Actually I had noticed that a certain relief all seemed secretive and got all the plum 'special-duty' jobs at dances and football matches for extra cash, long before the days of paid overtime. Welcome income, especially for young coppers on low pay.

'Aye, I see what you mean Brian.'

'Yeah, well, it's the only way to get on kid, marching up and down with your breast bared and trouser legs rolled up.' I laughed.

'Is that what they do?'

'God knows, far as I'm concerned they're overgrown boy scouts, but powerful ones who have a strangle hold on the job. You'd better learn all their bloody handshakes and stances and start talking about Boaz. Throw them into a right panic.' I was still naive.

'Or you could always join the Knights of St Columba.'

'What the hell's that?'

'Catholics kid, the opposition. It's either one or the other.'

'So which are you?'

'Nothing! I'm me kid, nobody can snap their fingers and get me running.'

I was shocked to think secret societies could wield so much power on the force. It seemed wrong, so I borrowed library books, and began observing my colleagues. Brian had been spot on; it was remarkable the number detected as members. I ended up having one or two verbal confrontations and can understand how my views were perhaps a bit disconcerting. The truth was I had no objections to anyone being members of anything, it was the 'secret' aspect and potential discrimination that got me. In later years several colleagues opened up completely, an attitude far more refreshing than in those early days.

Brian taught me how to enjoy the beat, highlighting how the public can be a rich source of wit and used this as a light innocent distraction. Like the time a tramp in Clayton Street West was rifling through litter bins.

'Aye, so what's going on here then?' Brian slid the words out.

'Nothing sir, nothing, just out for a walk sir.' A sad, innocent, harmless character.

'A walk eh? Well can you supply me with the current password?'

'Password sir?'

'Oh yes my friend, surely they've given you the password?' Brian looked at his watch, 'It's curfew time, after ten.' He furtively, drew him into the conspiracy. 'By rights, my associate and I should arrest you.'

'Curfew? Password? I didn't realise … honestly sir.' The man was panicking. Brian turned to me gravely.

'What do you think Mac, does he look honest enough?'

'Oh I think he's an honest man, Brian. He deserves a chance.' Brian turned all official.

'It's a good job my friend here is church going. All right I'll give you a chance. Now repeat the password after me.' The poor soul stood to attention while Brian made him repeat the password three times.

'The Count is having kippers with my grannie tonight!' All the while Brian's face remained impassive and I was just about rupturing myself holding in the laugh.

'Now then my friend, go about your lawful business, but if any police officer stops you, you must repeat the password. Do you understand?' The tramp nodded and gave a smart salute.

'Well done … now before you go about your business, my friend, please accept this gratuity for a hot cup of steaming Bovril,' and gave him a couple of bob indicating I should do the same. After my experience with Muscles, I didn't dare refuse.

At bait time some of the cops talked of tramps all over the city, stopping them and repeating unintelligible remarks which they insisted were a password for the night. Brian looked at me and twinkled, but never once enlightened them. Similar light relief was also experienced by filling a milk carton with water, placing it in the centre of the footpath, then hiding in a nearby shop doorway. Early morning workers couldn't resist giving it a hefty kick and Bang! Splash! The water would scoot up their trouser legs, while we were giggling out of sight. Did someone say we were protecting the public?

Brian's influence was permanent. He taught me to deal with the public in a sympathetic, helpful way, to be conscientious and above all thorough in my work. The art of cultivating informants from any given situation was also gleaned from him, and brought to real notice when one day he took me into the gents toilets in Clayton Street.

'Come with me kid, I'll show you a real character.'

'In this smelly place?' Brian smiled and led the way. The toilets were immaculate and a face appeared at the office window at the far end. He beamed when he saw Brian, obviously excited by the visit.

'Hello Brian, do you want to use the facilities?' He fumbled for his pass key.

'No it's all right Tom,' then turned to me, 'Good lad, Tom, always keeps the end bog here for his friends. Won't catch anything off the seat in there. You could eat your dinner off it.' Tom puffed his chest out with pride.

'Any time son, don't forget.' I just looked, but it registered, for clean public toilets were few and far between.

'Right Tom, kettle on?'

'For you, always Brian,' and led us into his office, shuffling papers off his desk and pulled two chairs up, at the same time switching the electric kettle on. All the while he fussed and obviously proud we were there.

'Still singing and dancing, Tom?' Brian winked at me.

'Yes, I try to keep my hand in at the Oxford Tea Dance.'

'Well what are you waiting for? Show Mac here what you can do.' Immediately Tom moved into the main urinal area and began singing and dancing 'Mammy … mahammmy.' It was embarrassing, but Brian kept encouraging him by joining in with the odd words and swaying. I wanted to crawl from sight because customers began to watch. Tom finished his 'act' and waited for the applause. Brian gave and then turned to the customers.

'Well clap you bastards. Clap!' And they did!

It certainly made Tom's day and we repaired to the cubby hole to enjoy our tea while he told us his life story. Before the war he had been in show business on the boards and after the war stage work had been difficult, so he had become a bin man. Then he had worked his way up through the ranks, finally in the latter stages landing this plum office appointment. A proud man and Brian showed a real affinity and care towards him. What I had originally thought was 'taking the piss' was not in fact so. One of the facets of Brian' character was you never really knew when he was kidding. Tom's toilet became a regular call after that. The kettle was always on and he became a mine of information, worth his weight in gold, a special constable – special, that is, to Brian and me.

Cultivating 'snecks' was an art, places such as cabins or boiler houses. Shops, offices, Chinese cafes, dance halls, pubs, workingmen's clubs, cafes and cinemas. In fact, anywhere where there were people. It made you get round your beat to get warm, a cup of tea or on some occasions even a sleep. It was by far the finest way to obtain local knowledge which was vital if you were to keep on top of your beat. Some sergeants hounded you and attempted to prevent you visiting such places, but theirs was an impossible task. Thankfully, through Brian's in-depth training I adopted his style and generally it worked. The art was to say little or nothing, but use your presence to maximum effect. For example a classic Brianism would go as follows.

'How are you doing honey?' The old crow behind the sweet shop counter would immediately respond; it must have been years since a tall handsome stranger in uniform had called her honey.

'I feel fine.'

'I was just remarking to my friend here what a pleasant woman you are. Always a smile for the customers. Being on the beat I notice these things.'

'Really?' The flattery completely disarmed her.

'Would you like a packet of cigarettes?'

'No honey, but a cup of tea and a chocolate digestive would be nice – to keep my bowels open.' It never failed, they all loved his patter.

Chinese cafes were a regular port of call for most beat men. I was fascinated by the smells, noise and nimble fingered cooks who could produce gastronomic mysteries at the drop of a hat. Marvellous places to observe a culture, so different from ours. Inscrutable to the end, their bland faces hid true feelings and little did I know that many years later I would live and work in Hong Kong and get to know these people so much better. A regular place in Northumberland Street involved climbing greasy stairs in Vine Lane, which were treacherous, but the jabber, sizzle, heat and fried rice were well worth it. I got to know the owner extremely well and he would regale his exploits at the gambling tables, which eventually bankrupted him.

One quiet Sunday afternoon I was creeping from this bolt hole when I bumped into three young boys struggling with a sack. 'Now then boys, what you got there?' They all coloured up.

'Come on now, what is it?' Still no answer, so I pulled the sack open and plunged my hand in, quickly withdrawing it as I touched something soft and fluffy. The three lads looked decidedly sheepish and as I opened the sack further revealed about twenty pigeons with the necks wrung. 'Oh aye?'

'Sorry sir,' the eldest spoke.

'Sorry? This is terrible. Why have you killed them?'

'We get a shilling each for them sir, from the man in the cafe,' pointing to the restaurant. I couldn't believe my ears.

'Let's get this straight, you sell them in there?'

'Yes sir, we've been doing it for weeks.'

'Weeks?'

'Yes sir, all the cafes take them. They mix it with chicken.' I was shocked and of course my enquiries proved negative, the Health Authorities came up with nothing, but my manager friend used to smile when I called after that. 'Piece of pigeon pie Mac?'

Another refuge was the cinema and apart from seeing the film it was also a great source of indecency merchants. You only had to stand at the rear and within minutes the seat jumpers could be spotted. Hopping like busy bees, either putting their nasty hands up female apparel or stealing handbags. I saw 'The Longest Day' at the Queens about twenty times and 'South Pacific' wasn't too bad either. The Olympia on Northumberland Road was always good for lock ups. Basically it was a flea pit where drunks slept off their morning session. A particularly horrible incident occurred when a notorious town drunk made his presence felt. He had hundreds of convictions and in drink was extremely violent. Often toerags would ply him with drink then stand back to watch the sport. You always knew when this character was ready for action because he would remove his teeth, snarl and strip off his clothing demanding to fight the street. Pub managers would hide as soon as he walked into their premises and immediately telephone the police in blind panic.

The usherette at the Olympia was certainly no match for him and when she refused him access he grabbed her skinny arm and snapped it over his knee. A cowardly attack for which he was given a short term of imprisonment, which, to him, was nothing but water off a duck's back. The usherette's life was never the same and I recall the anger I felt because real justice was not done. Over the years I arrested him several times, and as I got to know him better realised he needed medical help, but the system didn't provide a safety net. One afternoon I was standing at the Haymarket when I heard shouting and sure

A wonderful warm 'sneck' on a cold late turn. I remember seeing Bill Travers in 'Geordie' – an inspirational film.

enough there he was staggering, shouting and waving in my direction. Suddenly he stumbled in front of a bus which ran over his arm. There was a sickening crack and scream! Retribution had been exacted on him as I had witnessed both ends of the story, but a strange twist was to come. Not long after I was standing at the Bigg Market police box when I saw him stagger into the Chancellors Head Pub, bang on ten thirty. The Bigg Market was a centre for trouble, fights, prostitutes and low class pubs. A place to go if you craved action. Muscles nudged me. 'He won't be long in there mucker.' We watched and waited, waited and watched, eleven o'clock came and went, but no sign of our man. Ken and I hurried into the bar which was totally empty except for staff sweeping up. They gave us no more than a cursory glance.

'Where is X?'

'Who?' The blonde boy sweeping the floor laughed, 'Never seen him for years.' Ken's neck was bristling.

'Don't get funny with us mister he came in here over half an hour ago.' They completely ignored us, there was certainly no love lost.

'Right mucker, let's find him,' and we started searching, much to the staff's annoyance. The manager, a nasty individual, began shouting.

'I've told you he's not here, can't you guys understand English?'

'Well what's this?' says I, bending under a bench seat near to the door. There, squashed in, was our man unconscious. Ken and I dragged him out and only just appeared to have signs of life. His face was navy blue and had a fresh lump on his brow the size of a hen's egg. An ambulance came and en-route to the General Hospital he stopped breathing. Ken and I looked at each other in apprehension because the thought of mouth to mouth was revolting, so we began pumping his chest. I opened his mouth to ensure his teeth were not jammed in his throat and saw something right at the back. Grabbing the object I yanked, and out slid a full set of black boot laces. Some evil sod must have dropped them into his beer. The rush of air nearly sucked us in and as soon as he recovered began to cause trouble. The hospital refused treatment, he became so violent we were forced to arrest him. Our actions in saving his life were of no consequence whatsoever. We found out later the manager had attacked him with a shillelagh as soon as he'd walked into the pub, but could never prove it.

The drunk was a real Jeckyll and Hyde. Sober, a complete gentleman, and, in his cell, would always have his clothes neatly folded and be fully apologetic. I can still see his personal effects, an old tattered photograph of him in his army uniform and an elliptical tin of Brilliantine – nothing more! He regarded Durham Prison as a second home and was a model prisoner. I once bumped into him in reception pouring the teas out. He was genuinely pleased to see me.

'Are you still training Mac?'

'Aye.'

'Well stick this in your skye, good luck son' and pushed a huge slab of cheese into my hand. I hadn't the heart to refuse and still remains a pleasant memory of a man who sort of became a friend despite the odds.

SECTION SEVEN

BAPTISM OF FIRE

Forty one years ago at Holy Saviours Church,
Tynemouth – and we're still smiling. Little did Irene
know what she was letting herself in for.

Within a year of being married we moved from the damp flat in Akenside Terrace, Jesmond to a semi detached in Gosforth on the outskirts of Newcastle. Irene wanted to live in North Shields near the family, but I eventually persuaded her Gosforth was a better bet. It was pure chance buying the house we did. In the early hours of yet another damp nightshift I met up with Bob Anderson on the opposite beat, in Tilley's cafe doorway, Northumberland Road. We were calling the bosses as usual when he said, 'Do you know anybody who wants a house?' My ears pricked up.

'Yea, me actually.' Within minutes, without even looking at the property, we agreed on a price of £2,300. Later that day we went to view, and two days later a mortgage was secured.

It was tight, the mortgage was £13 10s 8d a month and I was only earning a little over that, but I had sworn never to move into a police house because if we did the force would own us lock, stock and barrel. Fortunately Irene was working at the Ministry of Pensions and making more than me, so while it was a struggle we kept our heads above water – just! Moving in with a few sticks of furniture gave us a fantastic feeling of security and independence, but that was soon shattered. We'd only been in two weeks when Irene woke me urgently in the middle of the night.

'Mac, I can smell smoke.' I turned to go back to sleep. Irene became distressed and began shaking me.

'Mac! The room's filling up with smoke, get up, get up!' Reluctantly I clambered out of bed and could hardly get down stairs. The smoke was so dense, and the lower living room was a blazing inferno. Panic set in, I was completely in the buff and dragged Irene outside in her night gown clutching Suki our Siamese cat. Foolishly I dashed back to save some money hidden in a tin in the living room – all the savings we had in the world. I managed to retrieve it, but the smoke and heat was intense, I couldn't breathe and staggered into the kitchen clawing at the back door in desperation. I was so desperate I ripped the door, plus the bolts from its moorings and fell coughing into the garden. It was amazing I managed to achieve such a thing, when all I should have done was release the bolts. Recovering a little I went to the front where Irene was shivering with the cat.

Peering down the street I thought I must be dreaming, for there was a fire engine extinguishing a fire at a petrol station garage. It was half past four in the morning. I ran down, still naked and grabbed a fireman.

'You'd better come up the street pal, my house is burning down.' The fireman smiled and turned away, he must have thought I was an escaped from nearby St Nicholas' Mental Hospital. I shook him violently.

'I'm not kidding man, it's bloody on fire.' He realised I was for real.

'Howay lads there's another one down here.' Within minutes they were crawling into the house with breathing apparatus and chopping axes and our chairs and settee were thrown from the window. The house was wrecked and twenty years later we were still suffering. It took months to eradicate the smell and every time I visited a house fire on duty could completely identify with the victims and the trauma they were experiencing.

Investigation showed the cause of the fire was a perished electric cable which had sparked on a gas pipe, which then ignited. The cat had saved our lives and the leading fire officer said that another five minutes and we would have been overcome by the fumes and died. Other people's problems I could relatively take in my stride in a cool collected and professional manner, but when it happened to me I panicked. No magical powers whatsoever.

Another incident confirmed this a few years later when my three year old daughter went missing. The knots in my stomach and the fear and dread completely overwhelmed both Irene and I for several hours. I reported her missing, but as a serving cop I was more aware of the

Our house fire made the local newspaper.

He ran for help—and found the brigade o

CONSTABLE'S HOME D

BLAZE AT GOSFORTH

A POLICEMAN dashed out of his blazing home to get help and found a fire engine almost on his doorstep.

Twenty - two - year - old Constable Arthur McKenzie said: "I was amazed, but it was lucky it was so close."

The firemen were just finishing work on another blaze at a garage 30 yards from Constable McKenzie's home in Glendale Avenue, Gosforth.

They went straight to the house and confined the blaze to one room.

"Apparently they had been at the garage for some time but my wife and I slept through all the noise," said Constable McKenzie.

Short circuit

"If we had been woken up, we might have discovered the fire in our house much earlier, because it seemed to have been burning a while."

His wife, Irene, woke when smoke seeped into an upstairs bedroom of the semi-detached house where they have lived for only a month.

"When I opened the living room door I was met by a wall of flames," said Constable McKenzie.

The blaze started under the floorboards.

A short in an electric cable is believed to have ignited escaping gas.

Furniture, carpets, wallpaper, the ceiling and the floor were damaged.

Flames lick garage tank

It was Mrs. McKenkie's 22nd birthday, and as she stood outside her home talking to firemen, she discovered that one of them was also celebrating his birthday.

They shook hands and exchanged good wishes.

Paraffin

In spite of the damage, Mrs. McKenkie was still able to have a quiet family tea party.

The first blaze, at Glendale Avenue Garage, destroyed the front of the building, including the office and all the papers belonging to the manager, Mr. Robert Redpath.

At one stage, flames were licking a tank containing 250 gallons of paraffin.

"It looked pretty nasty for a time," said Mr. Redpath.

One of a fleet of taxis parked in the garage was scorched.

In a third fire in the Gosforth area, floorboards and skirting, a carpenter's bench and timber were damaged in an attic workshop above a house in Moorfield Road.

Constable McKenzie and his wife, Irene.

dangers lurking in the streets. Coppers are naturally more over protective towards their families as are the keepers of the keys for many horrors. Much to our relief she was found playing nearby, but a picture of her little body lying somewhere had been uppermost in my mind throughout. I completely understood how others must have felt in similar circumstances and always endeavoured to deal with their situation thoughtfully and gently.

* * * * * * * * * * * * * * * * * * *

'If the public see you laughing kid – they'll think the job's a goodun.'

Funny, you rarely see a policeman laughing now – even the puppet in the glass case at Whitley Bay amusements has long become a collector's item.

Work was never motivated by promotion because I loved apprehending criminals. Each day I dreamed up new schemes to catch them. I had a theory that many villains actually enjoy the thrill of the chase, but none relish incarceration. Lady luck does play a part in success, but you also have to create your own luck. Eyes, ears and the other natural senses are vital, but above all else your judgement must include calculated risks. I often wondered if the public would sleep as soundly at night if they knew what was really going on in the streets. To my mind, it seemed there were criminals in every nook and cranny just waiting to be apprehended.

In the early 1960s transistor and car radios were the 'in' thing to nick and the City offered rich pickings indeed. Late turn (2 pm – 10 pm) there would be rows of unattended parked vehicles as cannon fodder. It's surprising how quiet it was at seven o'clock at night and my usual method was to look for an open motor then lie concealed in it. Often I would drive my own vehicle, an old Ford Thames van, or shin a drainpipe onto a shop roof to keep observations. I wasn't averse to changing into civvies or asking a shopkeeper for facilities after closing time. All was fair game and whilst some colleagues considered me eccentric, I felt it showed a degree of initiative.

My results bore fruit and I quickly learned to differentiate between opportunists and genuine pedestrians – something in their demeanour, body language, call it what you will. The sheer enjoyment of appearing from nowhere and firmly grasping a larcenous collar is an unparalleled buzz. Superintendent Joe Lowe seemed impressed and summoned me. In his high lay preacher voice he said, 'You seem to have a knack in catching thieves McKenzie?'

'I try sir.'

'Well, I'm putting you into plain clothes for a spell to see what you can do. Show the rest what it is all about. Lock up as many as you can.' Plain clothes! This was unbelievable, off the reins, a licence to operate as I wanted. Eager to show my paces, I redoubled my efforts and seemed to be falling over thieves in a spell which was lasted three months. Car thieves, burglars, shoplifters all caught in my trawl net. Unfortunately my headstrong approach incurred the wrath of the regular plain clothes squad who were all sweating on promotion to sergeant. Plain clothes was a natural staging post for promotions and classified as a plum job. In simple terms my volume of arrests not only embarrassed them, but threatened their cosy position. So they applied pressure on their sergeant, really stuck the knife in, and I was returned to uniform duties, but not before picking up commendations for good work. If instead of antagonism they had encouraged me they could have cashed in on my energy, enthusiasm and good luck, but it was not to be, and my hairy blue suit once more emerged from the wardrobe. Dame fortune smiled however, and I teamed up with 'Muscles' once more. A little older and wiser, we became such a strong entity we practically controlled the shift, and so began one of the happiest and most fulfilling years in my career.

'Blondie' was now station sergeant and he gave us our head. We lifted case after case from the streets and our approach engendered an infectious atmosphere. Other shift members began to compete and a feeling of comradeship was created. It was a pleasure operating with Ken, I would have done it for nothing. He had that ability to brighten the darkest day and help you to draw upon untapped abilities. We had our share of commendations from both Magistrates, Quarter Sessions and the Chief Constable, but Ken left me standing in the blocks on this score. Commendations are a bonus which occasionally come for the silliest cases, whilst circumstances where you may think credit is richly deserved pass you by and the following is a perfect example. At 4 am an early worker telephones to say a man is sitting on the pipes running down the outside of the old Redheugh Bridge. Together with sergeant Peter Marshall, and other police officers, Ken and I hot footed it to the bridge where we saw a man of about eighteen stone sitting on the outer pipe. He was rocking back and forward in pyjamas, trying to gain momentum and courage to jump off.

A plunge of one hundred feet and certain death lay below! Peter Marshall ordered us not to interfere, but his words fell on deaf, impetuous ears. It was a moral issue; Ken looked at me, 'Are you game mucker?' His face showed a steely determination.

'What do you think?' There's no way I would back out even though the sweat was running down my back.

Ken shouted, 'Hello there!' The man half turned, startled. Ken smiled his toothy grin and continued. 'Let's have a word fella. Look, if him and me come over and give you my hand will you collect it?' The man stared for what seemed an age, nodded, then looked absolutely petrified, shuffling about into an even more precarious situation.

'You stupid buggers, you're not going over.' Peter was worried!

'With respect sergeant.' Ken was not deterred and I followed. We clambered over the parapet, gradually inching along the two wide pipes running down the outside. These were a foot apart and extremely slippery in the early morning dew. Mist was rising from the river which

Redheugh Bridge – Muscles and I must have been crackers climbing over this.

looked grey, daunting and powerful. Ken and I said nothing, our actions were more important and the size of the man added to the problem. Gingerly we positioned ourselves either side and Ken reached forward with his hand. The man grasped it, mortally terrified, and began to panic. The atmosphere was charged as he slipped whilst attempting to claw his way to safety. His rancid breath and sweat added to the mix as we grabbed everything to hand, hair, shoulders, clothing. In the process my leg slipped between the gap in the pipes and I could hear Peter shouting, 'Let him drop! Don't be fools.' and I vividly remember seeing a carpet slipper float down as my face was pressed in between the pipes. The whole scene seemed to be in slow motion as the slipper bounced off a warehouse roof and silently landed in the river. Eventually our strength and good fortune managed to manhandle him to safety. The poor guy was a manic depressive, said he'd had a bad dream and woken on the pipes. Only one place for him – the mental hospital.

Ken and I were pleased with the result, but it was fairly commonplace for coppers to pull people from the many bridges spanning the Tyne. The sergeant submitted a short duty report and it was forgotten until a week later when Superintendent Jack Martin called Ken and I into his office.

'Why wasn't I told of this bridge escapade?' His temper was foul.

'The sergeant put a report in sir.' Ken grinned.

'Yes, well the bloody inspector didn't and, as a result, the two of you have missed out on a citation.' He went on to explain that because of inaction by the inspector, we would only have a special mention on our personal files. One of those things I suppose, but the irony is that particular inspector, nicknamed 'Goldfinger' because he had the unhealthy habit of continually putting his fingers up his backside to rearrange whatever was lodged up there. It didn't hold him back, however, for he went on to reach high rank. We later discovered he'd turned up in his car whilst the rescue was taking place, and, for reasons best know to himself, driven off at speed. The phrase 'lions led by donkeys' springs to mind.

From that moment events seemed to conspire against us and several complaints came in from hooligans and criminals wishing to deflect attention from themselves. Nothing serious, but tongues began wagging behind the scenes. Working cops are bound to ruffle a few feathers and supervisors began to worry in case it reflected on them. We were separated. I was placed in the upper reaches of suburban Jesmond and Ken on another shift thus ending a short lived era, but the experience was invaluable, and I'd like to think it made me a better policeman.

Unfortunately the stigma of impetuosity and rebelliousness remained with me the rest of my service. I could never shake it off. Individuals who did not know me believed wildly distorted exploits and where myth and reality clashed, myth always seemed to prevail. I learned to cover my back against some of the destructive forces within the service, but it never stifled my enthusiasm. Meanwhile my athletic career was developing steadily. Representation at County level meant travel throughout the country and this fired my ambitions to aim even higher. Work mates would smile knowingly if I talked of this, but their cynicism made me even more determined. Success bred success and eventually I secured the British Police Discus Championship in 1960 forcing the sceptics to take notice. Having this second string to my bow I was able to weather the storms as I bucked the system.

Returning to Jesmond, life was at a different pace, the beats consisted in the main of residential with very little vulnerable property. The boundaries were vast and this was in the days long before panda cars. So it was either shanks' pony or the beat bikes. Either mode was arduous and entailed physical fitness. Beat bikes? They were heavy as hell and only one was ever kept in reasonable condition – the sergeant's, and if you were caught using it there was hell to pay. One up from penny farthings they were to be avoided unless really necessary, because they made your backside red raw. We used to describe anyone riding one that they 'looked like a monkey on a mangle'. However I did find use for my 'mangle' in Sanderson Road late one evening.

I was pushing it down the street, attempting to look important, when suddenly there was a crash of glass from the bottom of the road. A mob of young men ran towards me, students performing 'high jinks' yet working men in the same situation would be called animals. As they approached me dodging left, then right, instinctively I hoisted the cycle over my head and threw it at them, trapping two squirming bodies against a hedge. Two lock ups! and I had to walk them all the way to Pilgrim Street, along with the bike. When the story became common knowledge I had some explaining to do to both supervision and the court, but I was secretly proud at finding a use at last for the dreaded metal.

Jesmond was a haven of 'snecks,' hotels and nursing homes

Cartoonist DUDLEY HALLWOOD was at the Billingham Games on Saturday.

I make the newspapers again – this time as a caricature.

probably the best. The latter were comfortable and the grub terrific, but there was a downside as you were often called to assist in laying out the odd geriatric who had passed on in the dark cold hours. The undertaker always called at the back door, a taxi no one ever calls for themselves. Homes of this type always saddened me, obviously borne from necessity, but from my observations most of the poor buggers were just waiting to die. I would often reflect if I would eventually become a resident of such a place. One night however it became obvious the copper was required for more than just a chat.

'How about something to keep you awake Mac?' The nurse was a dyed, dark haired beauty of around fifty, her false teeth bobbed in between the lipstick and smile.

'Coffee would be smashin' thanks.' Naive as hell!

'Why not take a couple of these?' She slid two purple hearts across the table, 'If you think you're fit wait until you take those.' The twinkle in her eye made no secret of her motives. I couldn't handle it.

'I'll have to go, got to ring in,' she raised her painted eyebrows.

'No, there's no need, you can use the phone here. Take your coat off, relax. All you ever think about is work.' My shirt was sticking to my back.

'The other lads look after me, why not you?' That was it, I was up and off, never to darken the doorstep again. Conversation in the refreshment room gravitated to the subject.

'They tell me you lost your nerve the other night puff nut?' George, an old reprobate better known for his drinking predilections than police work was taking the piss.

'You do realise you're spoiling it for the rest of us.' George was nasty in drink, offensive, sometimes violent. Best kept at arm's length.

'I don't want to talk about it right? Purple hearts and wrinkled boiler nurses are not really my scene.' George growled in my face, the smell of beer almost knocked me over.

'You might be thankful for a wrinkled old nurse and a couple of pills one day son.' It was a real eye opener, but cops are human beings and can be as weak and corrupt as councillors, builders, politicians, doctors or dust bin men!

* * * * * * * * * * * * * * * * * * * *

'The test of character is whether you'd let him follow you into the witness box kid.'

The job bounds with cynics who will spot the flaw in a character in a nanosecond. From day one if you're unlucky you'll be branded with a nickname which will stay with you for life. Here are examples of some of the most popular:

The Bugler – An inspector renowned for 'beating the retreat' whenever he was faced with hostility.
The Show Jumper – A detective who every time he went into a pub would have a clear round.
The Olympic Flame – He never went out (of the station).
Van Gogh – He had the gaffer's ear.
The Gannet – Would eat anything put in front of him at rapid speed.
The Turkish Blobseller – Who sneaked around as if he was trying to sell some dirty postcards in the Casbah.
Crazy Horse – Self explanatory.
The Eye Specialist – Every thing he said was prefixed by, 'I've done this … I've done that.'
All Strokes – When asked who could swim at the Training School, he put his hand up and said, 'I can do all strokes sergeant.'
One Eye, One Ear, One Arsehole – His number was 111.
The Cobweb – No way could you get him out of the corner.
Pluto – Who looked and spoke like the cartoon dog.
And so it went on.

Standards of policing should be above reproach, but it was a sad fact of life that whilst the majority of my colleagues were terrific, solid human beings occasionally I had to work with some despicable characters. It cut across all ranks and one particular sergeant was well known for his 'peeping tom' activities. He made my flesh creep, and that is exactly what he would do, creep and peep and his nocturnal slitherings knew every slack curtain and 'couples corner' in the division. Park shelters were his favourite haunts and he would regale his spying activities with great gusto and there was no doubt we were on a collision course. It came to a head in Park Terrace at the commencement of a night shift.

'You!' The tone was designed to unsettle me, but I was ready.

'Yes sergeant?' Monotone, staring hard, the time had come. I had to be strong.

'Why didn't you report those wagon drivers in St Thomas Crescent last night? The were all facing the wrong way without lights. Those bastards are taking the place off you.' Okay, long distance drivers often parked in St Thomas Crescent, but they weren't doing any harm, or causing obstruction, but he hated motorists. I responded, respectful to the rank, but not the man.

'Sorry sergeant, but I don't see what harm they're doing.' He braced, pulling his flabby body up and his voice took on a menace. My hackles were well up now, there was no way I was going to let him speak to me like a dog.

'Listen, I'm putting you on paper for neglect if you don't get down there and summons the lot. You're a slacker.' The rest of the shift saw sparks were going to fly and an older, wiser cop ushered them out, leaving me with the sergeant. This old sweat stood at the door. He didn't like the sergeant either and was an extremely shrewd bugger. Knowing I had support I turned to my aggressor.

'Okay sergeant, if it's cards on the table I'd better warn you if I ever catch you pimping on my patch I'll lock you up and make sure you fight me all the way to the station.' He'd been riding me for some time, what the hell. He turned puce, started to shake and I thought he was on a wobbler.

'Cheeky bugger, who do you think you're talking to?' The cop at the entrance winked. I swear if the sergeant had made to touch me I would have decked him, but externally I remained calm and came up with a response he could never have dreamed of.

'Okay sergeant, you want the lorry drivers summonsed. Fine by me, tell you what, if you saw them, and they were committing offences, you do them and I'll be your witness.' I had him by the short and curlies, but there was more, and I pulled a piece of paper from my pocket upon which I'd scribbled the numbers of twelve wagons.

'And to make it easy for you … here are the registration numbers.' There was a long pause as I put the paper on his desk.

'Now if you don't mind sergeant I've police work to do.' and pushed past him and into the fresh night air. He never ever bothered me again because he knew I meant every word, and years later I actually became his boss, then not long after that supervised the arrangements for his funeral.

Whispering Brian Hardie had taught me always to stand up for myself, no matter how heavy the brass or scrambled egg. It was brought home one Sunday dinner time after we'd enjoyed a pint in the 'Globe' off licence on Clayton Street. Wiping the froth from his tash he said, 'Walk straight out kid, no skulking. The better the face you put on, the more likely you are to get away with it.' So out we went and Bump! Right into the section sergeant Dick, nicknamed 'the bullet' because his number was 303. Dick was okay, but could have mood swings and had hands like hams. His dark hair, smart uniform and demeanour could be off putting, but underneath it all was a heart of gold and he looked after me in his own fatherly way. Being caught coming out of a pub was a disciplinary offence and I thought we were well and truly captured.

'Afternoon sarge.' Brian never flinched and gave his little smile. Dick edged closer in order to sniff our breath.

'And where have you two been?' The tone low and searching. Undeterred Brian fired back.

'You know fine well sergeant, for a pint.'

'You admit drinking on duty?'

Brian continued, 'Of course, what about it? You've had one today, why should we be any different?' I couldn't believe my ears, this had to be the finish, fined or even worse. Dick gave a pregnant pause, and a deep breath.

'Okay, I'll chalk your books here, but don't let me catch you again.' Scribbling in our books he moved away ramrod straight. Brian giggled, but said nothing. He didn't have to.

The shine was wearing thin as I was beginning to see dark corners, and disenchantment really caught me when I suspected an officer working the adjoining beat could be 'bent.' A burglar, and active as hell. Ostensibly hail fellow well met, he would curry favour with the sergeants and at first glance was a fine upstanding man. Very soon the whole shift were talking and it caused a great deal of unrest. We all suspected, but couldn't prove anything. Should we inform the gaffers? On face value he was an efficient cop, always ready to assist the public and my first encounter was six o'clock one morning as we were finishing.

'Lift son?' He had a brand new Morris Thousand and the rest of us had to walk, but a lift was helpful and he was going my way.

'Yea, ta,' and got into his motor. He suddenly remembered something.

'Just a sec,' and walked to a low wall surrounding the Exhibition Park, picked up a newspaper wrap and placed it in the boot. Wheezing he climbed in and from my look felt he owed an explanation.

'A few rose cuttings,' placing some of secataurs into the glove box.

'Best friend you could ever have, them.'

'Roses?'

'Aye, I recycle a few from the unoccupied houses. They'll never miss them. I was shocked, he was telling me he had stolen them.

Impossible to push it to the back of my mind, later that week I spoke with a colleague Ron. A very serious minded man he wasn't in the least surprised and confided that he too suspected the worst and had informed the sergeant. Eventually CID put him under surveillance and caught him red handed breaking into a series of offices in Grey Street. He admitted many other burglaries and was quoted that if he had been able to turn another cop he could have taken the town away. I often wonder if I was ever in his sights to be propositioned? Nothing is worse than a bent cop. It creates poison in the force, morale plummets and public confidence is severely undermined.

Patrolling Jesmond was pleasant, but as a residential area at holiday times most of the shift was spent checking unoccupied houses. If a house was broken into or insecure and we didn't discover it, reports would fly for months. I always attempted to be conscientious, but on this occasion wished I hadn't been so keen. The night in question I'd was checking a residence in Highbury overlooking the Town Moor. A corner property, it was intact around eleven but as I passed at one thirty, I decided to examine it again. An eerie place, it was screened by high bushes, plus it had a long crunchy gravel path. I opened the wrought iron gates and crept along the grass verge. As I approached, I noticed a ground floor window slightly open and immediately the adrenaline pumped as I moved forward and peeped into room, just in time to see a hand closing the door behind it. My mind was in turmoil. We didn't have radios and heart pounding I galloped for the door, gathering momentum with each stride. Bracing my shoulder I hit it 'Crash!' It flew in and I kept going, clean through an inner glass door, then careered on knocking over a telephone table, hat stand and vase. The noise was horrendous, added to which I ran round the house shouting, 'Got you, you bastard.' Searching under beds, in wardrobes, on all three floors. Suddenly it dawned, the room where I'd seen the hand? There was no such room, only a passage wall. The dread hit me, I rushed into the garden where my fears were confirmed. The window to the left of the door was for a house round the corner where lights were shining. Bloody hell! Suddenly a man came running from that house shouting, demented.

'Quick, come quick, there's burglars next door and my mother has had a heart attack.' If only I could have become instantly invisible. Fortunately the old lady survived, but I had to nail up the front door. It would have been cheaper to have had burglars! When the unsuspecting owners returned from holiday a few days later I was waiting. They stared in disbelief, but appreciated the attention if not the damage. Of course my stupidity became a real source of jocularity with the rest of the shift, but looking on the bright side, I could have caught myself a bloody good burglar.

Jesmond was truly beautiful, especially on a winter's morning a soft virginal carpet of snow everywhere. You could see for miles and I seemed so at one with nature. I derived pleasure in following animal tracks in the snow to locate where their nocturnal wanderings took them. Basic instincts make you aware of a life to which we are oblivious. Spring mornings a revelation, with flowers and trees at their best and half drowsy black birds swooping low, tugging at worms from dewy lawns is thrilling. Nature is in control, not man, and coming face to face with its powerful and arbitrary decisions over life and death can be a very harrowing experience. Two experiences spring to mind. The first was on Jesmond Road in the early hours. A large fluffy Persian cat had been run over and lay gasping on the footpath. I knew I had to put it mercifully out of it's misery, but where and how? Carefully lifting the soft ball, I carried it to Barrass Bridge where the new Civic Centre was being built. En route I met Geoff from the adjoining beat.

'What are you doing?' He looked visibly upset.

'I'm going to put it down.'

'What? No, can you not leave it. It'll be all right man.' Hope sometimes springs eternal, but not in this case.

'No chance Geoff. Got to be done.' I laid the broken body on the building site placing its head on a brick. Geoff looked away as I selected a large stone, stroked it fondly, its blood ridden eyes looked at me and I knew it understood. Then speedily I did the deed and Geoff broke into tears. I felt terrible and deciding to give it a decent burial dug a shallow grave with my truncheon beside a large tree next to the

A police band at the newly-built Civic Centre. Peddler Palmer played the drums and George Cooper the euphonium. Marie Hope – the singer – is to the left behind the stooping sergeant. A touch of class playing in the new – and by the same token sounding their own death knell. I find it difficult to say anything positive about the Civic Centre because to me it is symbolic of the destruction of what was a fine city. A monument to everything that was the 1960s.

Civic Centre foundations, marking the spot with a crude wooden cross. The grave remained visible for months and I always sought it out as I passed on the bus. Even now when I look at the monstrous Civic Centre I consider it to be a fitting tombstone for the cat.

A similar experience involved an injured dog which I had to take to the Cat and Dog shelter on Claremont Road. It was closed and the animal beyond redemption. I asked my partner, 'Pass the humane killer.' A cartridge loaded gun which fires a short spike a few inches was handed by my mate. Bang! The dog flinched and moved causing the spike to glance off its skull. It screamed, leapt from the rear of the van, stumbled and dragged its way onto the Town Moor. After a hectic chase we were forced to kill it with our sticks. I shudder to think what any potential witnesses may have thought. A gruesome tale, but necessary action and it made me violently sick. Being a copper was surely a job of contrasts, but that's what made it so interesting and repelling.

I have watched slaughtermen at the Cattle Market abattoir and marvelled at their skill, but wondered how they could take life after life, one after the other. I would look into their eyes and wonder how fine the line was between killing an animal and a human being. Mortuary attendants are yet another group. You got to know them quite well, because death became part of your life. One day I had been in to take particulars of a sudden death when the attendant at the RVI stopped me on the way out.

'Ee I wouldn't like your job son.'

'Eh?'

'Not very nice is it? You must see some awful things.' I smiled,

'Yes, I suppose you're right.' He handed me a blood stained newspaper wrap of violet cuttings.

'Give these cuttings to Toddy the Coroners Officer will you?'

Incredibly he was giving me new life in the shadow of the old – unforgettable images.

IT'S A NITTY GRITTY WORLD

Pilgrim Street Foot, 1964 – before it was vandalised. I can see the promotion ladder going away from me at a rate of knots.

Creatures of the night

Peeping Toms are more prevalent than most people would like to recognise. Pathetic, lonely characters, but the potential damage to their victims can be disastrous. A pair of hidden eyes devouring your most private moments is abhorrent and distasteful whether the voyeur is harmless or not. Hunting them is extremely difficult, they all have territories, and when interviewed can give you the most remarkable details about individual habits. Some of their antics in satisfying their lust to spy were mind boggling, no window inaccessible or grass too short as they snaked along on their bellies to watch couples in the park. As for the fear factor I had first hand experience at my own home which made me all the more determined to bear down upon the offence whenever I had the opportunity.

Returning home at 2 am off half nights I found Irene crying and trembling, mortally terrified. Her story tumbled out. She'd been sitting knitting when Suki, our cat, had moved to the French windows, gone behind the curtains and started mewing. Irene pulled the curtains apart and there pressed against the glass was a pale face. She reeled back in horror, but had the presence of mind to switch the lights off, run upstairs and look out of the bedroom window in order to get a better description. There was no sign of the intruder, so after a few minutes of trembling she returned downstairs, then heard a slow knocking on the back door. In panic she ran out the front door which slammed behind her, then rushed blindly to a neighbour's house. When the police arrived the intruder had escaped.

I was alarmed and angry, and had never seen Irene so frightened, so I made a determined effort to catch the intruder. I set a trap, placing a small stone on the inside base of the door. Over the next two weeks I examined this stone regularly and found it was being moved. There was also a fresh heel mark in the soil outside the back window so I knew pale face was back and determined. I didn't tell Irene, but night after night I maintained vigil from the front room with the light off, sitting well back in the shadows. Nothing happened for a few days, but I was patient. I planned on allowing him access to the back garden where I would drag him through our sharp beech hedge in the ensuing fight – then arrest him. My emotions were running high. Being a copper didn't enter into it. Irene couldn't sleep at nights, and I was hell-bent on paying him back for the misery caused.

Weeks passed, still nothing. Then one night some relatives called and left about eight. As they walked down the front path and we waved our goodbyes I decided to have an hour's obbo. I'd just settled into the front room, when a shadowy figure stealthily crept from the back lane opposite wearing a long coat and cap. I saw his face as he passed under the street lamp and knew it was my man. Breathing through my teeth I watched him slide up the path, looking both ways, then go to the side door. I had previously nailed it up and he displayed annoyance when it wouldn't open even after putting his shoulder to it. Failing miserably, he then attempted to climb over and as he did so I hurried out in my carpet slippers for stealth and touched him on the shoulder.

'Can I help you pal?' He turned, and the fear shone from his eyes.

'Bastard!' I shouted and punched him full in the face. He dropped like a felled bullock then seemed to gather, sprang back up and grappled with me. I had lost it totally by this time and Irene came running to door drawn by the noise. As soon as she saw us she began screaming.

'That's him Mac. That's him!'

'Get the police.' She was rooted to the spot.

'I can't come past him.'

'Phone the bloody police!' She inched past and ran to a neighbour. Our struggle continued and waiting for the police seemed an eternity.

Eventually a police car pulled up and a fat sergeant jumped out. I didn't know him because we lived in Northumberland outside of Newcastle, so it was a completely different force. He grabbed me by the neck and pulled.

'He's had enough!'

'Enough? I haven't started yet.' I was really annoyed at his approach.

'He's had enough I tell you.' Then turning to my prisoner said, 'Right lad on your way and don't let's have any of this again.' What the hell was happening? He was letting him go.

'I want him charged.'

'No need for that, just a minor offence.'

I was livid. 'Look mister, I'm a copper myself and if you don't do your job properly I'll take him to the station myself.' The lazy sod didn't want to know, but as soon as I told him who I was he changed.

'Oh I didn't realise.' My prisoner was reluctantly taken away. I was shaking with emotion and astounded at the sergeant's attitude.

Eventually the peeping tom was charged and admitted many similar offences in the district, turning out to be a part time voluntary mental patient at the nearby hospital. The sequel was a little disturbing for when he appeared at court he pleaded 'Not Guilty' and the defence levelled an unprecedented attack on me. The sergeant certainly hadn't done his job properly and I explained to the court in my own words exactly what had happened, including my violent response in defence of my property and family. He was convicted!

For many years my wife and I both had dreams about that man and it preyed on our minds. An unnerving, but sobering experience.

* * * * * * * * * * * * * * * * * * *

Becoming a grim faced detective

In 1962 my career took a dramatic change when I was transferred to CID as an aide. This was a brand new experiment in policing as prior the route into this prestigious department was through service, strong recommendation and contacts. But this was the sixties and experimentation was being tried everywhere so I became an apprentice detective moving to the West End, scene of my earlier explosives

A grim faced Drugs Squad Detective leaving the Collingwood Clinic, Gosforth, in the mid 1970s

triumph. The surroundings were unfamiliar and working in civvies I quickly found I wasn't a super cop. West End detectives had a reputation for being tough, uncompromising and classified as the best in the force.

Within days I fell foul of a detective sergeant who had a most unfortunate manner operating as the office Godfather, bullying everyone with his puffed up importance. Those who worked with him were frightened and I always had the impression he had power, but from whence I knew not where. Anyhow, we didn't see eye to eye after I had submitted my first file to him. A simple larceny of a driving licence and the young criminal arrested eventually became a force target in later years. I'd tugged him on the street, turned up the licence and felt it was a good starter for ten. Little did I know what I was in for when I reported for duty at five o'clock, both shifts intermingling in the office.

'McKenzie,' his voice boomed up the office and I scurried forward.

'Yes sergeant?' He sat omnipotent in his desk at the top of the office.

'What do you think this is?' waving my carefully constructed file.

'File for larceny sergeant.' He then set about belittling me in front of the office and by now everyone was watching.

'Load of shite. You'll never make a detective as long as you have a hole in your arse.' My face burned as he tore my file into shreds. I had this urge to chin him, but bit my lip and took the abuse. The torrent went on for several painful minutes and I vowed I would have my day with him. From that moment on he made my life a misery, putting me on diabolical shifts. The 3 am to 11 am milk token theft patrols were his favourite, so my athletics training went right down the tubes. I'm still at a loss to understand why he took such a dislike to me.

I was unhappy and aspirations of making the British Athletics Team were rapidly disappearing. After four months of this agony I was sitting in the office one night when I, took stock. Did I really wanted to be doing this? I wasn't part of the 'in crowd' and was still determined to retain my individuality.

'Sir, I wish to return to uniform duties forthwith.' The report I drafted was succinct.

'I'm not signing that,' said Peter, another detective sergeant in the office. He thrust it back.

'I'll push it under the DI's door unsigned if you don't.' Peter shrugged.

'Okay, but it's the worst day's work you ever did son and there's no way you'll ever be an international athlete, so you can kick that one into touch.' I smiled at him and had to take some stick from the rest because everyone thought I was foolish for opting out of a prestigious job. A decision I had to live with for several years. Every time I went on interview it was held to my head like a gun, but it was the best move I ever made. Not only did I make the British Athletics Team, but returned to the West End on two successive promotions, settled my score with the Detective Sergeant who'd set out to make my life a misery and ended up the boss. So much for their judgement on my ability as a detective or athlete.

* * * * * * * * * * * * * * * * * * *

Bigg Market and other battles

I returned to my old hunting ground in the city, back into uniform. The superintendent was pleased to see me. Nicknamed 'Whacky Jacky,' a volatile old buzzard, only wanted work and knew I was prepared to supply same. I explained my athletics prospects and volunteered to work permanent early night (6 pm – 2 am) in order to have a regular shift which enabled me to train during the day.

1963 was my magic year. Irene expecting our first child and I was knocking on the door of the full British Athletics Team, carrying off all championships and getting stronger through progressive weight lifting. Others thought I was mad volunteering to work the Bigg Market, probably one of the most infamous spots in Newcastle. There I would

'You'll never make an International Athlete as long as you've got a hole in your arse.'

Even though Arthur McKenzie (Big Mac) was a field events man, and I was a middle and long distance coach, our paths crossed many times. Arthur was, and still is, one of the most enthuasistic people I have ever met. In 1970 he was ranked 3rd in Great Britain's All Time list for the discus which was achieved at the Commonwealth Games in Edinburgh. I reckon that his most remarkable record is that he still holds the Championship record for the Discus in the North Eastern Counties Championship. At 32 years this is the oldest record in the book.

Arthur and I collaborated in bringing the story of James Rowan (the Black Callant) to public attention. Rowan was forgotten by the public for over 100 years. World champion at 6 and 10 miles, he was only 7 stone 8 pounds and stood 5 foot 4 inches tall. He died in poverty at 28 years of age. Arthur took up the cudgels for this forgotten hero and has written a screenplay based on Rowan's story.

I consider Arthur a jack of all trades and master of most, a good friend and great company.

Stan Long

stand, a solitary figure, waiting for trouble at the Tardis police box. It came every night, and the excitement was terrific. It also pandered to my ego, my own patch again and seemingly in control of it. Nightly I arrived home battered and bruised, but it was enjoyable and taught me to fend for myself at an even higher level. More importantly I made a lot of friends and earned the grudging respect of several villains which stood me in good stead later. Many hated my guts, but tackling them on their own territory was important, even if I didn't win all the battles.

Andrew Mark McKenzie was born in May 1963. I was a proud father. A feeling of elation only matched, when, in June the same year, I received my first full international vest in the discus. All trials and tribulations had been well worth it and the sceptics made to eat the words. Now with a family, I began to consider my actions more carefully, where before I had stepped in where angels feared to tread. Life took on a completely different hue, I became more mature and responsible. Nevertheless, I still continued to enjoy my fair share of unavoidable fights in the Bigg Market. Sergeant Ossie Old, conscientious to a fault, met up with me one night at ten o'clock.

'All quiet Mac?'

'Yep,' but the words were hardly from my lips when a fight erupted twenty yards away. We ran over and Ossie was attacked, two of them jumping on his back, dragging him to the ground. Ossie had only recently come out of hospital after a hernia operation so I stepped in. His attackers were a couple of gypsies out for a night's sport. I managed to contain them and force them into the police box, my strength being the biggest factor. By then another fracas had begun and two of them were rolling and fighting on the ground. I leapt onto one of their backs and pulled his hair hard, digging into the greasy roots. Shrieks emitted from the man on the ground and my prisoner spat

Irene and Andrew at Sandringham Gardens, North Shields, Christmas, 1965. The little lad went to bed in that cowboy hat for months.

something into my face as I manhandled him to the box. The other man continued to scream and with good cause, for my prisoner had bitten the end of his finger off and that was what he'd spat at me. My tug had effectively ripped the other man's finger off.

Biting seemed to be the 'in' thing and I nearly had my nose bitten off in a fight when I was out with 'Muscles' when arresting a hot dog man in Pink Lane ... fortunately he failed, but the most stark incident occurred weeks after Andrew's birth. It was the first opportunity Irene and I had to go out and my mother baby sat whilst we went to the pictures. We went to the Odeon, 'Bye Bye Birdie' was showing, and we sat in the back row downstairs. After a while I noticed Irene kept moving closer to me and it wasn't passion.

'What's the matter?' She said nothing, but I could see something was amiss. I said, 'What's up pet?' She suddenly blurted it out.

'Mac, the man next to me has his hand on my leg!'

'Get out, Irene!' I dragged her past me, stood up and lashed out hard in fury into the guy's face. His head bounced off the plywood at the rear of the row, then he unravelled and turned out to be larger than me in every way. We locked and a vicious fight commenced during which I was unable to secure a firm hold on his short leather jacket which stunk. Other patrons began screaming as we plundered along the row, he desperately trying to escape, I holding on for grim death. We rolled into the foyer where he suddenly latched onto my right ear with his teeth, snarling and shaking, trying to tear it off. He was growling like a mad dog, the pain excruciating, I thought my ear was a goner. Desperately I jammed my thumb up his nose several times, splitting it wide open, forcing him to release his molar grip. I quickly followed up with a crude strangle-hold and we crashed to the floor.

The foyer was in full commotion, a large crowd gathering and Irene screaming as she could see blood spurting from my ear. He seemed to have the strength of ten as we wrestled and writhed for what appeared an eternity and several times he was within an ace of escaping. I was constantly shouting for assistance when the under manager stepped in, dinner suit, bow tie, the lot, and attempted to drag me off.

'Stop it! He's had enough!'

'I'm a polis you idiot. I'm arresting him. Send for the bloody police!'

'You'll have to pay for any damage. The responsibility's yours.' What the hell was this tailor's dummy talking about?

I desperately shouted at him, 'Phone for the police you idiot.' I pushed him in the chest, he staggered backwards and half demolished the sweet counter. Within minutes four cops ran in through the entrance, after all the station was only thirty yards away.

'It's Mac,' one shouted. The subdued under manager began shouting his apologies. It took four of them to manhandle my prisoner, struggling like a zebra to the station.

He was charged with indecent assault on Irene and wounding on me and served a total of nine months in prison. His list of convictions was extensive, almost all of them for indecency inside cinemas, the last whilst he was sitting with his own wife. Truly one of the evilest and most dangerous men I have ever encountered in my service. Again Irene had been a witness to police work. Fortunately my ear, hanging on by a thin piece of skin, healed!

Violence runs as a common thread through most copper's service. It was stock-in-trade and performing duty outside dance halls at week ends could be tense affairs. Mob violence outside the Majestic, Mayfair and Oxford Galleries was always on the cards, and many a cop received a beating at such venues. John Gregson Garrett took over as our shift Inspector and addressed us in the parade room.

'Where there is trouble, gentlemen, you will always find me,' and he couldn't have been more right. The following night he was pushed through a plate glass window outside the Oxford and fortunately came out unscathed. John Garrett was the epitome of smartness, proud of his rank, a fraction pompous, but straight as a die, and, above all, reliable. He always backed his staff, a quality lacking in so many others and by far his biggest asset was he would always be in the rough and tumble.

Despite his traumatic experience, a couple of nights later I found myself outside the same dance hall with him. It was midnight and you could smell violence in the air. Drunks milling everywhere, trying to 'score', taxi drivers jostled for business and the whole scene permeated by a smell of hot dogs. Then it kicked off; a plastic receptacle containing tomato ketchup bounced off a taxi roof and burst, covering myself and the inspector with its foul smelling contents. John grabbed my cuff and held me back.

'Now then Mac, stay calm.' I was livid and scanned the sea of grinning faces.

'Come on son, keep steady, we're above this.' He tried to placate me, but I spotted our assailant, now with the mustard container and his arm drawn back with a challenging grin on his face. He hurled it and miraculously I managed to catch it in mid flight and set off after him, dragging myself away from the inspector.

'Mac, Mac, leave him.' His words were left in my wake. We had been made to look stupid and I was going to mete out the remedy. Forcing my way through the boisterous crowds made it difficult, but they also hampered my prey. Determined, I made a full length dive outside the BBC studios and pinned him down. Again a red mist was up, I opened his mouth and squeezed as much of the mustard as possible in, forcing him to swallow it in gulps. Dragging him to his feet I formally made my arrest and then fate took over, showing just how lucky I was and unlucky he was.

At the police station I searched him and discovered four purses, all stolen from the dance floor. A native of Portsmouth he was also wanted there for a series of crimes and again my impetuosity had resulted in a corking case.

'Good lad Mac.' John Garrett marched into the station covered from head to toe in ketchup and patted me on the head like a dog.

Bailed for court, the thief failed to turn up so a warrant was issued for his arrest, a warrant in which I took great interest. I left it a couple of weeks then on a quiet Sunday morning, visited the address he'd given on arrest. Malvern Street in the West End, a run down, seedy bed-sit. At half past seven the door was opened by a skinny girl under twenty.

'Is he in, pet?' I brushed past her without an invite, but she knew the score. The smell of stale air, dirt and poverty made me retch.

'He's gone back to Pompey,' but I knew her eyes were lying as I searched the room. In the centre was a cot containing a young child and a large Alsation dog lying full length, both fast asleep. Unable to find my man the girl began regaining her confidence and turned uppety.

'See, I told y', coming here, waking innocent people up. I'm going to complain against you.' My eyes caught a movement as the wardrobe shook slightly, or was it my imagination?

'Aye, is that right pet?' I turned to walk out, at the same time pulling the wardrobe over, crashing it to the floor. Shouts and a hollow bumping noise emitted.

'Pompey eh?' She gave up and walked into the passage as I lifted up the wardrobe and extracted my prey. The dog leaped from the cot barking and snacking, the baby began crying. The man shrugged and smiled.

'You can't blame me for trying,' and laughed, we both laughed. I was chuffed I'd seen it through from A – Z. Not a major case, but one which underlined the fulfilment and enjoyment I derived from the job.

* * * * * * * * * * * * * * * * * * *

It's people, not things that are interesting

Early turn was a bind, and I normally made duty by my eyelashes. One Sunday morning I was rushing into Pilgrim Street at five past six when I spotted two men shuffling uncomfortably outside, one elderly, the other obviously his son. The police station was empty except for a telephone operator wandering through with a cup of tea.

'A couple of guys outside look as if they're going to give themselves up,' I said to the operator who wasn't the least bit interested. Operators generally had a misplaced sense of power and this man was no exception, a real snake who snouted for Fergie. He left me alone as the two men hesitantly came through the revolving doors. The younger pushing the older one forward.

'Go on tell him.' The old man was shaking like a leaf.

'Now then dad, nothing's that bad.' I smiled to relax him.

'I've just murdered my wife and shot her lover!' I thought my ears were playing tricks and looked at the son who nodded, fear in his eyes. I tried to remain calm, but inside was extremely excited. This bloke was giving himself up for murder!

'Yes, well we'll try and sort it out,' and took them through into the charge room where the station staff were enjoying a chin wag and cuppa. Sergeant Nick Carter and I took them into the interview room where the old man collapsed onto the table. His son spoke again.

'My dad's also taken two bottles of aspirins.' Nick looked at me with a glazed expression, what the hell was I bringing in now? A double murderer who had tried to commit suicide. Nick, a nice bloke, remained calm and said, 'Aye, well, we'll just have to deal with it,' and deal with it we did, one of the smoothest cases I was ever involved in.

Right enough, the guy had shot his wife at a caravan park in County Durham after seeing her with another man. After killing her at close range with a shotgun, he forged a note in her handwriting, asking the lover to meet in a secluded spot. Demented, he hid behind a bush and upon hearing footsteps blasted the gun off again. Fortunately he missed and whoever it was we never did find out. He'd certainly taken an overdose and I accompanied him to the hospital where I assisted the nurses with the stomach pump. Not pleasant. When he came round he looked terrible and I helped him sit up, then clasping my arm said, 'We've had a hell of a day you and me son. Thanks for everything.' Despite his heinous crime I felt sorry for him and the facts unearthed a classic 'crime of passion' and he was sentenced to seven years for manslaughter. At seventy it was an awful way to spend the final years of his life.

The bizarre can be an every day occurrence and eventually begins to pass over your mind like air.

'Officer there's murders on down the road.' Late shift, about seven, and a member of the public called for my assistance. I strolled to where the noise was coming from, Leazes Terrace, in the shadow of St James' Park. From a downstairs flat an old crone rushed to intercept me.

'It's him, he's found another. I'm going to kill him,' she must have been eighty and dressed in a diaphanous creation as if she was awaiting a curtain call for the music hall. Lipstick like Bette Davis in 'Whatever Happened To Baby Jane,' powder an inch thick, and piggy little eyes glaring at me. She looked just like a Geordie Geisha. Leading me into the musty passage, a man slid from the shadows. He had long hair parted down the centre, quiff either side, large bushy eyebrows waxed to points and a moustache to match. Staring like some occult goat, he was unintelligible. They stood side by side – what a pair!

'So, what's the matter?' I wish I hadn't asked because as the story unfolded I found out they were mother and son who had enjoyed an incestuous relationship most of their lives. This was one of those occasions when discretion was definitely the better part of valour, but she insisted on showing me the 'other woman' and led me into the front room.

'I've given him the best years of my life, and this is the way he repays me,' clawing at my sleeve with a scrawny hand pulling me into the gloom.

'There she is, all smug, look at her. I want her out! Now!' I gazed around the room, there was no one to be seen.

'Who pet? Who?'

'Are you blind? Her!' To my horror I realised she was pointing to a large cat sitting on the piano, blinking at me, or was it winking? No

Leazes Terrace. Another magnificent piece of architecture which has fortunately been saved and transcends the shadow of St James' Park.

way was I going to make an investigation, I could just imagine if I took this team into the station and demanded a doctor's examination. In time honoured way I made an excuse and left as quickly as my legs would carry me.

Eccentrics seemed to seek me out and often I would have to clear evil spirits from a house, especially those with a propensity for photographing unsuspecting victims on the lavatory. Either that or rays beaming through the walls. I often had to smile, but never took the mick despite the obvious comic content because Muscles words always came back to me.

'It could be you one day mucka.'

* * * * * * * * * * * * * * * * * *

Back to real work – I loved it!

Permanent early nights in the Bigg Market eventually caught up and became self defeating. Every night I was 'locking up' and having to appear at court next day, leaving little time for training. As a member of the British Team I was pushing for higher honours, and regular training was vital. Once again I approached Whacky Jacky. Supportive as ever, he suggested a spell on days and posted me to Pilgrim Street foot where a huge building regeneration project was being carried out. They were tearing down the Royal Arcade and building a motorway and roundabout complex. My arrest-rate plummeted and I had more time for training, but the job became permanent point duty. Frustration set in, because I still craved the hurly burly. My patience ran out after three months and despite a desperate attempt to qualify for the Olympics in Tokyo I wasn't selected and as this had been the prime object for day shift I requested a further return to shifts.

That spell made me rusty as a policeman, and luckily I saw the danger signs. I was young, still with hopes of a future, but on my return to shifts it was Fergie the station sergeant who greeted me with a gravestone look.

'Earlies starting tomorrow. You might be able to twist the super round your little finger, but not me, so remember before you tappy lappy to him again, you go through me. I'm your gaffer. Understand?' For a split second I wondered whether I'd made the right move, but stood my ground.

ARTHUR McKENZIE—success in career and athletics.

P.C. 430 WANTS TO CAPTURE TOKIO TRIP

IF Arthur McKenzie, one of Britain's three top discus throwers, is chosen to go to the Olympic Games, thanks will be due in no small measure to Newcastle City Police.

For P.C. 430 McKenzie often trains in spare time allotted to him by the Watch Committee and the City Police.

When he goes to Welwyn Garden City on August 28 to take part in the British Specialist Trials at which prospects for Tokio will be chosen he will carry the good wishes of the Watch Committee with him.

COMMENDED

Arthur is the force's top all-rounder. Not only is this 25-year-old policeman one of the country's best athletes, but he is fast making a reputation for himself in his chosen job.

In five and a half years he was won four commendations—one by the Chief Constable and three from the City magistrates.

Northern Counties discus champion for the last three years and an international competitor for two, he now has his eyes set on the "big time."

He will represent the Northern Counties Athletic Association in shot events in the A.A.A. Championship on July 10.

EXCELLENT

If he does well he hopes to be selected to represent Britain against Finland at Helsinki from July 21 to 24.

He may also qualify for a place in the team to meet Hungary and Poland in August.

A senior officer in Newcastle police said of Arthur, whose home is in Glendale Avenue, Gosforth: "It is quite rare to have a policeman so excellent at athletics. We have certainly never had anyone so good."

Not to be – but what the hell. Being out on a summer's evening on your own, smelling newly-mown grass and throwing the discus was the nearest thing to heaven.

'I'm a polis sergeant, I'll work anywhere, but even if you are my boss I wont be spoken to like a dog.'

'Cheeky bastard, you better keep your nose clean otherwise I'll bury you without trace.' He didn't have to tell me.

'Goes both ways sergeant.'

Fergie turned on his heels and I knew the gauntlet was down. It didn't take long and when on early shift I was late, sure enough Fergie put me on report. It was my fault, I was put on paper three times in a week and warned should it happen again I would be in front of the Chief Constable.

Determined to keep a clean sheet, next morning I woke bright and early at the crack of dawn. Washed, shaved, a good breakfast I was first into Park Terrace as the night shift went off duty. Smugly I sat reading reports. I'd cracked it and bristling with enthusiasm when my colleagues crawled in.

'What's the matter, can't you get up in the mornings?' They weren't in the mood for my jokes. I was fresh as paint, which wasn't so surprising seeing I'd been in bed at seven the night before. Ossie rang the shift in and duties were allocated to everyone – except me.

'What are you waiting for kidda?' Ossie maintained a dead pan face.

'My duties sergeant.' He then spoke slowly and methodically.

'Stupid bugger, you've come to work on your day off!' Bloody hell ... I couldn't believe it and I had to return home feeling a right pillock and I certainly had to take some stick from the rest of the lads. Early day and me weren't compatible because I was so tired from my training. Often I'd arrive for duty resplendent in full uniform and brown shoes. I once came in a red tie, carpet slippers and without my cap, and was forced to walk the beat like that. Fortunately I balanced this side of my nature through sport, which gave me credibility and far more important my flair for arresting thieves was still there. Returning to shifts meant relieving beats which gave plenty of variation and prevented staleness. I enjoyed being a free agent and able to operate with wide parameters. Thirst for the hunt was back with a vengeance and it seemed every time I reported for duty a thief would be there for the taking. One of the most comical of these involved my penchant for sleep.

Training through the day sometimes involved two punishing work outs which meant by midnight I would be dead beat, so if things were quiet I would find somewhere to have a quiet snooze. Open cars were favourite, but the City Stylish on Newbridge Street had a pleasant, warm doorway. The frontage had a gate which could easily be removed, then replaced, affording complete privacy. To the left was a small alcove where I could lie wrapped in George Bone's finest overcoat and fold the cape as a pillow. Pure, luxury! On this particular night I'd checked the patch and was in for second bottle (2 am) so I decided on a nap. In no time at all I was well wrapped and quickly slipped into that twilight zone, but hazily aware of the outside world. Suddenly I jumped, startled, it wasn't a noise, but a sensation and sitting bolt upright my heart was pounding furiously. I focused into the gloom at the tailor's dummy in the window and thought there was something odd about it. Then I realised it wasn't a dummy, but a burglar with a crowbar in his hand. He'd been forcing the rear display when I'd walked in for my somnambulant interlude. He came like a mouse.

'What's the charge officer?' Fergie stood on ceremony, glasses down his nose. He had this habit of looking over them.

'Shopbreaking sergeant.'

'Where's your evidence officer?' I chose my words carefully.

'I captured him screwing City Stylish with this,' holding up the crowbar.

'Why don't you tell him you were sleeping in the doorway bastard!' Fergie looked hard at me.

'Is that right?'

'Sleeping?'

'Bloody ask him!' The burglar was enjoying it.

'Depends if you believe a thief before me, sergeant.' There was no way I was going to cough and it made no difference to the evidence. Fergie wasn't pleased, but let it drop, but I knew given half a chance to do me he would in like a rat up a drainpipe.

One of the biggest traps of all on the police force is drink. Most of us enjoyed a pint, but the temptation of a free run has ruined many police officer's careers and lives. I used to enjoy the odd one in the snug on late shift in the Haymarket just prior to terminating duty, but always did my best to be careful. Yet I probably stumbled upon one of the finest cases in my career whilst 'under the influence.' One late turn I teamed up with Jackie Bell, the first ever dog handler in Newcastle. The week had been extremely successful and I'd had good lock ups every day, so chatting with Jack was relaxing for he had a great sense of humour.

'Howay son, we'll take the dog round the bars and snarl at a few prigs (hooligans).' Jack was a raw boned country lad turned Townie and his booming voice made everyone stare as we strode through the pubs showing the flag. Police dogs were a great topic of conversation and Jack was past master of eliciting a pint. He could swallow like a horse and I found it difficult keeping pace. Pints kept appearing, five, six, seven, I began to waver and was frightened to lean forward in case I drowned. At quarter past ten I realised that it was way past my finishing time.

'I'll have to go Jack.' His muscular face broke into a smile.

'Okay son, I'll hang on for another hour to give the dog its exercise,' and I tottered off to hear him shouting, 'Take the back lanes son.' The last pint that night had been in the pub at the corner of Darn Crook and West Walls (St Andrew's Street). I staggered along the cobbled lane beside the Ancient city walls where I was forced to relieve myself. Feeling dizzy I headed towards Cross Street box taking all the time in the world, when suddenly I heard BANG! A tremendous noise, similar to a car back firing. BANG! Off it went again and sounded like it was coming from Low Friar Street. In a haze I peeped along the street which was silent as the grave except for a shadow twenty yards on the right opposite La Dolce Vita Club. My scrambled mind was working erratically, but decided the shadow was human and calculated he must be kicking in the rear door of the Strand Outfitters. I skulked along the wall and grabbed his shoulders.

'What's on here then?' Something glinted in the darkness of the doorway and I realised there were two of them, the other one facing me and pointing something. I grasped it before he respond then realised I was holding a revolver. The drink and adrenaline came in real handy as I tucked it into my tunic poacher's pockets without considering the consequences. I began dragging them to Cross Street police box, fifty yards away.

My senses told me that they would attempt to escape for they kept looking at each other. Arriving at the box I realised my difficulty because the box key was attached to my whistle chain in my top left tunic pocket and extricating it and holding onto my prisoners created a huge problem. I was forced to release one of them and they both stood still as the key was placed in the lock. That was the signal, each bolted in opposite directions leaving me suspended from the end of my chain. Wrenching free, I chased after one, caught him and the other surrendered when he saw his mate captured.

They had stolen the firearm from a parked vehicle outside a gun club in the Haymarket and firing it along Low Friar Street to see if it worked. Had I been sober no way would I have stumbled upon or indeed tackled the situation as I did. One of the ironies of police work seemed to be, if you were skiving, time and again you would drop on a transgressor. It often happened to other coppers and any worth his salt would be hard pressed to say he never had a drink on duty. The old prints characterising rotund, red faced coppers sipping a mug of beer in the maid's parlour are days long gone, but I was fortunate enough to catch the tail end of that era. Jack had been one of them and sadly I never saw him again for he died not long after.

'Set a thief to catch a thief,' is one of those pieces of para-wisdom favoured by nanas, club secretaries and retired Yorkshire cricket umpires, but although his idea of a Saturday night well spent was a bus ride to Wallsend in search of a 'rumble', a la West Side Story, Arthur McKenzie has always been honest and fair, qualities that have not always been to his benefit.

In the days when the equivalent of 'community service' was a slap across the lug from the leather gloved palm of the local 'bobby' by some accident of fate, this young tear-away from North Shields found himself being fitted for a pair of the aforementioned gloves and all the other trappings associated with our boys on 'The Force', and this is where the stories really started.

Arthur is the first to suggest that he is no 'Billy' Shakespeare, (then again, some say that 'Billy' Shakespeare wasn't 'Billy' Shakespeare), but he skilfully tells his tales with a clarity and with the natural honesty that is this big man.

Davey Whitaker
Thespian of this fair city

I SWEAR BY ALMIGHTY GOD

Holding this up was far easier than the Scales of Justice.

It's one thing to process members of the public and arrest villains, but court is where a cop stands or falls and learns an important facet of his trade. Once again Muscles and 'Whispering' Brian Hardie taught me where the Venus fly traps existed. Probably the biggest is in you own mind for unless you have certainty in a case it is wrong to be in court in the first place. Whatever justice or injustice occurs within the four walls of that strange world should be of no consequence to an officer provided he has performed to his level best. Each appearance adds a building brick of experience, and on no account should the courts of justice be treated with familiarity. Court was described to me by a barrister as a stage, where the best actors triumphed for good or evil. Slightly melodramatic perhaps, but there was more than a grain of truth in what he said. I met good and bad briefs, but never allowed them to get under my skin and always attempted to give as good as I got. The only way to learn is by physical experience, feeling the sweat roll down your back whilst under pressure, yet retaining a cool exterior.

Apart from the serious purpose of court there were often interludes of humour within these vacuums of walnut and wigs. Quarter Sessions was the most embarrassing! As a young man I was summoned from my honeymoon in 1960 to give evidence in three separate cases, one the 'Omo and Daz' gross indecency trial, another, two men for possession of housebreaking implements, and an appeal against disqualification. I was keyed up for each appearance as it was my first real stab at high court.

'Calling PC McKenzie!' Heart in my mouth, wearing a freshly pressed uniform I rushed into the deafening silence of court number one with all faces pointed at me in expectation.

'Up the stairs officer.'

The court usher indicated the wooden stairs leading into the witness box. I thundered up eager to please then CRACK! My head hit the roof of the entrance with a sickening thud. The excruciating pain took away all worry of giving evidence. I got through it and gingerly returned to the well of the court, pleased it was over. No such luck, I was recalled to give a point of clarification and again ran up the stairs. BANG! Once more my head rattled on the roof raising a titter round the court and a huge bump on my head. I felt a right berk, but got through it and once more returned to the well of the court. After the jury's deliberation the housebreakers were finally convicted and I was summoned to give their antecedent history. For a third time I sprang up the stairs and this time the crash rang round the court nearly rocking it on its foundations. I fell to my knees, stunned like a bullock.

'Bloody hell!' I shouted and clutched my cranium. Court ushers dashed to assist and all eyes watched as I was given water and a seat. The judge, peered over his half glasses, the hint of a smile playing on his lips.

'Are you all right officer?'

I lied and said, 'Yes.'

Muscles was extremely well known throughout the courts by villains and magistrates alike, but one Monday morning he put me right on the spot. Mondays at the Mags Court in Newcastle were packed with accused, police, probation officers, solicitors. It almost bordered on a social occasion and often a pleasurable experience. You could spot villains for the future and likewise they would identify you to their associates. A legal sausage machine, with drunks wheeled through first, and within the court room it was literally standing room only. Muscles and I were at the rear of the dock leaning on the wooden surround whispering. The general hub-bub meant our conversation was relatively private. One magistrate, an enormous woman, seemed to be making numbers up for she said nothing. A bleary eyed drunk, head down in total dejection was waiting in the dock to be sentenced. The Chairman of the Bench began to speak.

'We will not tolerate this kind of behaviour, and take such a serious view of your case that we have decided to … '

He didn't finish, Muscles did it for him and in a stage whisper said, 'Run three times round the big fat magistrate.' And dodged down behind the dock. At that moment there had been a lull, everyone waiting for sentence. At Muscles' utterance the court broke up into laughter and everyone but the magistrates thought I had spoken. The clerk stared, I stared back, the pregnant pause lasted a full minute and then the proceedings commenced as if nothing had happened. A light relief and magic moment.

Drunks were bread and butter cases, falling into many categories. Some were arrested for their own good and others for the publics'. The worst example I ever saw was at half past six during an early morning cell examination. Lying on the floor covered in vomit and excreta was a pathetic bundle of life. The smell made a pig sty seem like an air freshner. At one end of the cell block was a large enamel bath so I ran it. The soap used was utility red carbolic, with the little boy on it, edges so sharp you could have shaved with it if desired. I placed it on the side of the bath, roused the drunk and led him undressed to partake of the waters. He was bent and twisted, his vertebrae sticking out like pegs -a walking skeleton. The soap had slipped into the bath and melted in the hot water so I leaned forward intending to run the cold tap. Before I could move my charge eased into the bath and lay there, never a word or noise and I couldn't even put my hand into the boiling water. Any normal individual would have received serious burns, but he was so physically deteriorated it must have anaesthetised him.

Alcoholics and drop outs normally came quietly, thankful for a bed, but each drunk is different and you never know who you are likely to grip. Called to the Haymarket one early morning a man mountain was smashing wing mirrors off parked cars. A twenty stone grizzly bear and roaring drunk. Scrambling from the panda car I attempted to remonstrate with him, but he brushed me aside like a fly. I responded, we grappled, a fight ensued and I found it virtually impossible to subdue this monster. Fortunately I managed to get a firm neck lock on him and my partner and I manhandled him into the panda car. Upon arrival at the station he wouldn't climb the stairs, where another fight ensued and after ten minutes he submitted, banging the flat of his hand on the ground. When he finally sobered he turned out to be a famous professional wrestler, having appeared at the City Hall that night – unbeaten! He implored me to maintain a low profile on his humiliation; terrified it would make the newspapers. Out of drink he was a really nice guy and I saw him on television several times after that where he gave the impression of being a real animal. I have to admit every time I saw him I couldn't resist a wry smile.

* * * * * * * * * * * * * * * * * * * *

Never let Police Work get in the way of your CAREER

1966 and all was happening again both at home and on the sports field. Irene was expecting our second child and I was sweating on an England place for the Commonwealth Games in Jamaica. As number one thrower in Britain, the pressures were enormous, so once more I knocked on Whacky's door.

'There's a patrol going at the Haymarket in a week or two. The man there is retiring. Take over after he goes.' And once more I found myself on regular day shift and duly reported to the Haymarket box.

Bill Gibson, the regular man, was a large bull of a man, respected by both colleagues and public. This dour Scot had broken a few jaws in his time and feared no one. He showed me the ropes, pointed out the tea spots and introduced his contacts. The place was well sewn up, every minute of the day accounted for. Bill had given thirty years to the job, every one of them at the sharp end and it was a privilege to work with him for a week. On the Friday lunch time he said, quite casually.

'Have you got your own car nearby big fella?'

'Yeah, it's in the University car park.'

'Any chance of a run home?' Of course it wasn't a problem, so I collected my V.W. and ran him up the North Road to The Blue House, an isolated police house on the corner of the Town Moor. I pulled into the lay-by on Grandstand Road opposite and noticed the slightest trace of a tear in his eye. He gave a firm handshake.

'Well, that's it Mac, I won't be wearing this uniform again.' I looked.

'Know what son? Nobody has said anything, not goodbye, not a word, not a handshake, it's as if I never existed.' Then smiled, 'But not to worry eh?' climbed out of my car, and waved goodbye.

Bill's last second on the job and I was there. This had happened before with Arthur Grimes in the Court Office, the sentiments so similar, confirming we were just a number. Thirty years and no one could even say 'thank you' was a really sobering thought. Some cops retire with a big booze up, where the professional bun fighters slap you on the back and tell you what a great guy you are. Behind all of that bonhomie however some are plotting and scheming their next rung on the ladder or destroying a career. Generally speaking they only slap your back because you are paying for the beer. Often retirement gatherings only confirm to the recipient he is surplus to requirements.

Some even moan if they have to subscribe towards a wreath when a colleague dies.

'Why should I? I didn't know him.' This was a side of the service I was never able to reconcile myself with, yet on the other side of the coin there were some marvellous pals who would move heaven and earth to help.

Paul Heslop, who I met whilst patrolling the Haymarket, fell into this category. A young cop who looked even younger, he was nicknamed 'Potent Paul' because at twenty two he had five children. Thin and weedy, he more than made up for it with tenacity and intelligence. I bumped into him at the box.

'They tell me you do a bit of training?' He flexed his bones. 'Think you could give me a schedule, I want to put on a bit of weight?' I gave him the once over and immediately took to him.

'Okay, but it's hard work.' He smiled, a slight caste in his blue eyes.

'I'm not frightened of hard work.' He said, and he wasn't. A close friendship developed, Paul put his heart and soul into training, but what is far more important he effectively changed my career and life in a dramatic way. One day in the gym at Jubilee School, North Shields, now the property of North Shields Polytechnic, he said to me, 'Why aren't you through the exams?'

'Exams? No way. I'm happy. Not interested.' This was true so far as it went, but I'd failed to make the team for Jamaica, having dipped out with three no throws at the trials at White City, London that summer. Probably one of the biggest disappointments in my athletic career especially as I was ranked number 1 in Britain at that time – but the selection process was cut throat – like life I suppose. Kirsty, my daughter, had been born so there other things on my mind than police promotion examinations.

A rare family photograph of Kirsty and Andrew as children with Irene, my father and mother-in-law.

'Look around you man. See all the plebs getting promoted. It's all wrong, you should be through. You owe it to your family.' He was right!

'Look, I'll study with you. You've helped me, so I'll help you. In fact I like studying like you like training. So how about it?' He talked so much bloody sense I knew I couldn't turn the chance down.

'Okay, you're on!'

Once committed we both went at it with all guns blazing and became fanatics at studying law. Failure to make the Games meant a return to beat work, and fortunately I shared the same relief as Paul. We became so knowledgeable, spending every spare minute with our noses in the books. This continued solidly for twelve months, and were so keyed up it wasn't a question of passing the exam, but aiming for top marks.

All the sweat paid dividends. Our marks were so high it qualified us for a paper sift for Bramshill Police College. The Chief Constable congratulated me on the results.

'Mac, you've shocked everybody here.' Then came the crunchers.

'Of course you do realise that you don't have the right background?' I was a mongrel, whereas high flyers must be pedigree and police ability had nothing to do with advancement. I'd gained one of the highest marks in the country, yet wasn't good enough, and this was compounded when a policeman at the bottom of the list made the Police College on interview. But by sheer chance his dad was an ACC in a neighbouring force!

Now qualified to sergeant I was a part of the system and came right under the microscope.

'Mustn't do this. Watch that. Your promotion is a stake. Keep in the gaffer's good books. Don't rock the boat.' Inspector Joe Scott had been right all those years before. Yes! the job did seem to be run by a 'League of Frightened men', but despite peer pressure I was determined to remain my own man and put promotion to the back of my mind.

Finances hadn't been good since the birth of Andrew and the arrival of Kirsty made circumstances even harsher. Police pay was a pittance and we struggled once Irene left work. She was forced to sell some of her clothes in order to buy shoes for the kids and I started doing odd jobs for friends and neighbours. Painting and decorating saved us from some severe difficulties. Of course this was contrary to the Discipline Code so I was leaving myself wide open, but it was either that or Social Security Supplement. Of course it didn't take long for an anonymous letter to drop on the Super's desk and I was forced to withdraw my moonlighting. I had my suspicions about the letter, but I left it at that.

Fergie didn't let the grass grow under his feet and was promoted Inspector for his last couple of years. As luck had it he remained on my shift. Daggers remained very much drawn between us and not only did we have a clash of personalities, but I objected to his oppressive leadership. In the final week of his service he summoned me to his office on nightshift. His desk littered with papers, he peered over his specs and I thought, 'Here goes.'

'As you know I'm retiring and you won't be unhappy about that will you young fellow?' I smiled. He wasn't wrong. I was delirious.

'You haven't called me in to tell me that sir.'

'No, you're bloody right I haven't. I want to keep the record straight mister. I've been going through the charge sheets and record books and you're featured in them more than anybody.' This wasn't the man I knew and loved.

'So I'm putting you forward for a Chief Constable's Commendation.' He peered over his specs, still condescending, but with a twinkle in the normally cold eyes.

'Thanks very much sir.' I was flabbergasted.

'Right sunny Jim, that's all,' stood up and shook my hand.

'And don't let the bastards like me grind you down.'

I left his office dazed, but happy. In my own way I had won, but he had the last word and removed all of the acrimony from our relationship. Like so many other men who I worked closely with I never saw him again … yet another to die after a short retirement.

My relationship with Whacky still remained friendly as I was attracting much publicity to the force through my sporting exploits. The Olympics were looking a distinct possibility, radio and television were taking an interest and life became more intensive. The thrill of the hunt was still a driving force and it was obvious I was gravitating more towards CID work. I would memorise all circulations for wanted persons and that attention to detail paid off handsomely one summer afternoon.

I had been to a strength competition at the Lightfoot Sports Stadium in the East End of Newcastle. Television cameras were in attendance and I had worked so hard I was worn out. On the return journey I was sprawled out in the rear seat of my mate, Peter Harper's car. Peter was National coach and looked after my training needs. I was propped up with my head on the arm rest of his Hillman Sceptre and we became snarled up in tea time traffic on Shields Road, stopping, starting, crawling at a snail's pace. My eyes wandered to the registration plate of a green A./35 Van in a side junction waiting to join our traffic stream. RSM 618. I repeated the numbers and suddenly realised.

'Christ! That's a stolen car, Peter.' Adrenaline pumping I jumped from the car and dashed across the road nearly being knocked over in the process. Yanking the door open I manhandled the driver into the rear and squeezed into the seat. A quiet young boy sat on the passenger side and the driver was shouting.

'What's this, a bloody high jack?' and began punching me about the head. The passenger then attempted to escape. Working on a full head of steam I grabbed the young lad by the hair then rammed my foot on the accelerator lurching into the traffic.

'I'm a polis mister, and this is a stolen car. You're both arrested.' The man in the rear picked up a wheel brace and tried to hit me across the head but thankfully the confined space smothered his efforts and he hit the roof. Swinging backwards I managed to sending him reeling. Several days earlier the collator, an early crime intelligence officer, had

Working out with police colleagues at Newcastle Exhibition Park
Summer Fair at the Police Stand – 'No weighting'.

passed this registration number on with the information it was
officially allotted to a Scottish tractor. In my wild, positive approach
both of the occupants lost their nerve and driving like a lunatic in
excitement I screamed into the station yard. It was a stolen vehicle all
right and both of them were wanted for an orgy of crime throughout
the North East and admitted at least fifty offences. The passenger
turned out to be a girl! A good job I didn't try to search her otherwise I
could have been up for indecent assault. Peter Harper was lost for
words, it had been impossible for him to follow my driving, but it was
a precious moment for both of us and a great pity the television
cameras hadn't captured that on film. As I was interviewing the
prisoners Whacky entered the room, stared at the thieves then patted
my shoulder. There was no need for words I knew he was proud.

Before tip toeing further mention should be made of the spin offs
gained purely from the streets of 'paddling the patch' as it was
affectionately called. I was always a bit of a romantic and loved to use
my imagination. For example I would love to meander through church
yards at night to read the gravestones and became totally absorbed the
stories they told. History recorded on the granite blocks, real events;
death from leprosy, black plague or 'shotte in Weste Walles for
desertion' it was there to see and I would try to visualise what life must
have been like for the people who once lived in the streets I now
patrolled.

'Hung on the Town Moor for stealing a handkerchief.' The Town
Moor! The heart and lungs of Newcastle! Cattle graze there and it is

tranquillity personified, but has witnessed many dramas. Rapes, murders, suicides, you name it! Located on the main trunk road, it performs important functions; providing the city dwellers a place to jog, go courting, or simply walk the dog. However the acreage had to be policed and I spent many windswept hours searching for lost children or rounding up stray cows. It also became the backdrop to a small, personal triumph.

Living in Gosforth I had to use the bus, but this short journey from Newcastle became a bind on late shifts. A particularly obnoxious local villain would regularly work himself.

'I'm not paying until he does, the slimy slag, bloody filth.' The tirade would pour, and despite my anger I would bite my lip. However there was a limit to the goading I could take and on this night in question he was particularly vicious. Other passengers were uncomfortable and I had to bite the bullet. I rang the bell and the bus stopped right outside the Town Moor main entrance. I dragged him off and waved the bus on.

'Okay pal, just you and me, about time we sorted this out.'

'Big man in your uniform eh?' I didn't hesitate, it was like going back in time to my first tentative steps on six beat. I peeled my tunic off and we set to both giving it our best shots and finally breaking even. We ended up puffing, sweating and walking across the moor together, the score well and truly settled. There was no question of arrest, the personal satisfaction was more than sufficient. I ran into him on several occasions during the course of my service after that and he always acknowledged me. Never a friend, but a firm acquaintance.

* * * * * * * * * * * * * * * * * * * *

More tip toeing in a tunic

By far one of the most successful forms of policing was the common or garden 'pull' in the street. Far from harassing the public it gave thieves slightly less odds of escaping detection, confirmed when I struck up a conversation in the police station with a young thief. I didn't know him from Adam, but he knew all about me.

'How come you know so much about me kidda?' He smiled.

'A relative of mine pointed you out in Eldon Square and told me to avoid you at any cost, especially if I was carrying anything dodgy because you would give me a pull. So if I see you I walk round the block.' Sobering words indeed! Of course the 'pull' demanded common sense. Random checks without reason were pointless.

After a while a sixth sense seemed to prevail, something about the demeanour or body language. Is he walking too fast or slow? Time of day or night and the clothes worn. Who would wear a top coat in the summer. In other words did it look that little bit out of the ordinary. Is he or she a known thief? Have you seen him at court before with a known thief? All of these factors were brought into the main frame to create a picture. Once the decision had been made it was important to

*Eldon Square – A monument to the brave, sadly now a large litter bin.
How quickly we forget.*

use diplomacy and tact and it taught me to be able to talk and think
quickly. Initially adopting the pleasant approach, provided room for
manoeuvre. If things turned hairy, you could say with hand on heart
that you'd done your best to be sociable. Again these stops could be
bizarre. Four o'clock in the morning, I'm standing in the Haymarket
when two women and a man passed me pushing a pram. Something
about the way they glanced at me rang a bell, but I allowed them to
walk on, then suddenly the man crossed the road and began walking
independently. There was no reason why he should have done that so I
ran round the block and headed them off. Sprinting through the streets
and back lanes I eventually stopped them on Barrack Road, outside the
gates to St James' Park, and there was no sight of the man.

'Now then girls, bit late to be taking the bairn out,' and peered into
the pram, but was prevented by its lock fast hood. They didn't reply, I
continued with a nice approach, but my nose was twitching.

'What you got in there? A safe?' Still no reply but I knew there was a
rabbit away.

'Where's the guy I saw you with earlier? Has he left you holding the
baby.' Suddenly the man leapt from the bushes.

'Here I am, what about it? We've just brought the bairn from
hospital.'

'Let's see then?' He stood defiantly in front of me.

'No you bloody can't, he's bad and we've got to get him home.' I
remained calm.

'Yea, well I'd feel a lot happier if I saw him for myself. For all I know
you could be an international pram stealing gang,' and laughed, at the

same time pulling the cover off. The man bolted, and little wonder because there was no child, nothing like one, the pram was filled with tins, bottles and foodstuffs. They gave up without a murmur and I got the guy later.

It turned out to be an extremely pathetic story, for the property had been stolen from a burned out store in Oxford Street and for sexual favours the night watchman had been allowing them entrance to steal at will. A dirty old man who ended up doing time. Searching their West End flat revealed that the man was living with both women and they had six kids between them. Poor little mites, all sleeping in one large bed, feet pointing to the centre like the spokes of a giant wheel. They were stuffed to the gills, their stomachs distended with the remains of Branston Pickle and meat on their fingers and lips, snoring, contentedly. Searching that house certainly tugged at my heart, for in every cupboard were large tins of ham, pickle, bottles of disinfectant and boxes of Swan Vestas matches. They must have thought they had made it for life poor buggers, but the food had to be removed because it could be contaminated, tins blown by the fire. I didn't have the heart to take the half eaten ham and jars of pickle on the table.

You had to close your mind to poverty, and whilst some of it is created by society much of it is induced by lack of education. There can never be any excuse for personal filth, and some people simply lived like farmyard animals. One such abode involved searching for a missing girl at a house at Newburn. I discovered her, one in the morning hiding in a sideboard in her boyfriend's bedroom. His parents were drug addicts and a young baby lay asleep in a pram in the passage. When I took a good look at it the sight made my flesh creep for lice were wriggling all over the little soul, in eyes, mouth and nose. A horrible sight, but more incredibly the baby never stirred.

Dealing with diabolical situations daily can turn a copper cynical very quickly, yet a smile in the most critical of moments costs nothing and can invariably remove tension. Sadly some cops become morose, developing a cold stare as if undressing you, miserable buggers, they are about as much fun as the bubonic plague. I found life was so much more interesting by talking to as many people from diverse backgrounds as possible. Some cops refused to talk to thieves, prostitutes and the like, somehow forgetting that these people also had hopes, fears and ambitions. Once I had dealt with somebody, as far as I was concerned the book was shut. Also every arrest is a potential informant, and the bigger the villain the better quality information you could get off them. Women made the better 'snouts' because they use spite as the motivation. Information was everywhere, all you had to do was to recognise it. Wandering the back lanes, I would often look through dustbins because they said a hell of a lot about the occupants of the house. For me catching thieves was always top priority, but it was always important to keep on the boil with the smaller cases. This in turn kept the senses alive, familiarity with the courts and paper work procedures, which were changing constantly. Once the sharp edge of participation was lost, regaining it was difficult to re-capture.

All I needed to keep the pot boiling was to walk up any main street, conceal myself within view of any large store and soon I'd have a shoplifter in my grasp. Easy pickings and all grist to the mill.

* * * * * * * * * * * * * * * * * * * *

The day traditional police work died

Introduction of the panda car system linked with personal radios completely revolutionised the police service and in many eyes killed us stone dead. The initial concept of instant communications and quick response appealed to both public and police alike, but within a very short space of time we realised that personal contact, which was so important, had gone. The police service had now become a car with a blue light whizzing past to deal with someone else's problem. A reasonably trained beat man could generally pin point problems long before they ever reared their ugly heads, but more importantly he could feel the pulse of the community. No way did I want to be cooped up in a Hillman Imp, so I volunteered to work Neville Street patrol. Like the Bigg Market it was hard, consisting of the area along the frontage to the Central Railway Station. Main source of activity came from the Victoria and Comet pub, affectionately known as the 'sick and vomit' and a watering hole for Irish navvies. These large red faced, barrel chested, curly haired individuals worked like Trojans during the day and drank like Brendan Behan at night. Generally speaking, 'the ganger,' would keep them in check, but they always presented a quiet menace. Turfing such rugged specimens out at closing time while separating them from drink was always a tricky business. No matter how hard you pushed they slid back as if on wheels. I quickly learned a shouting Irishman is no problem, it's the one standing quietly at the bar who will smash the bottle over your head given the opportunity. Prostitutes festooned the area plying their blousy trade and fleecing 'Paddy' or anyone else for that matter.

Irish labourers were mostly the salt of the earth, living for the second, but many times I was pleased to see the ganger appear at a confrontation. Neville Street was to be my last year at the sharp end in uniform, but it proved to be yet another excellent training ground. Street work was sadly drawing to a close, and a system that had remained static and tested for years was being fragmented. The street was a magic place, every second could be different. Where else could you move into such contrasting emotions within the space of a few yards, or meet such memorable characters?

Yes, those days were alive, interesting and exciting, but the death knell for Newcastle City Police was sounding when the force was swallowed in our first amalgamation in 1969. A City man and proud of it, overnight the whole atmosphere and structure of the force changed. Prior to the amalgamation there had been much jockeying for key positions. Whacky called me in.

'It's being considered to promote you to sergeant. Are you prepared to move home in this event?'

'No way sir.' and I wasn't, having lived most of my married life in the same house. My kids were settled at school and so was Irene. Promotion could have meant being transferred to Berwick or some dead and alive hole. I had joined the City and had no intention of tearing up my roots. Promotion didn't mean that much to me and I told him so.

'Your decision son, but it could affect your chances. I hope you understand that?' I understood all right, but wasn't worried. Another four officers had been given similar interviews and all agreed to move if necessary.

Come the amalgamation none of us was promoted, but understood we were on a list when the opportunity arose. Instead of sergeant's stripes I was transferred into the plain clothes department, which was way better than promotion anyhow. Dealing with vice, gambling, assaults, warrants, licensing enquiries we were generally the super's right-hand men. A small unit, laws unto ourselves with wide terms of reference. Tailor-made for me. I was ecstatic about the move. Our sergeant was Ossie Old and I teamed up with a young cop, Peter Leask. Together we made a frontal attack on vice problems, searching shops under the Obscene Publications Acts and dealing with offences of prostitution, gross indecency and all forms of assaults.

In the first six months of 1968 we arrested and convicted over sixty persons for a multitude of offences and those in the vice game knew we had arrived. Each week-end, along with Ossie we would visit the pubs to check on the pulse of the city. One cardinal rule was never to accept any drink from a manager that wasn't in a sealed bottle otherwise they would only give you the slops. One night in the Three Bulls Heads pub on Percy Street I found the local hooks playing darts on my photograph taken from the local paper. Quite amusing really, but it was all in good fun … or I think it was.

Vice enquiries radically changed my views because whilst on the surface this seedy side of life seemed to exist only fractionally, I soon found that once the stones were lifted the pond life wriggling underneath told a completely different story. In law an object or photograph could not be classified as obscene unless it had the tendency to deprave and corrupt, yet the law could not define this clearly. Some of the material I had to observe in the course of my duty poisoned my own mind and frightened me a little. Despite this, I always attempted to use rational judgement. It wasn't for me to be a judge or jury, and whatever prejudices I did have I kept them out of the arena. I got to know many prostitutes who were mines of information, and most of them, whilst clearly victims, retained a terrific sense of humour. Many were beaten and forced onto the streets by pimps, a subject I became somewhat of an expert on later in my service, but that is for another time and place. Whilst plain clothes days were happy, it was during this period I fell foul of Whacky who had been upgraded to Chief Superintendent and moved to Gosforth main station. The other four men promised promotion were given their stripes and I was the only one left out. Incensed at the discrimination for not agreeing to move home I submitted a controversial report saying exactly that.

It hit the fan one quiet Saturday morning in 1970. The telephone rang. It was Whacky.

'Get yourself up to my office NOW mister. You've got your wires crossed.' Now Whacky was king of the bollockings and my stomach churned as I walked through his office door. He immediately jumped up and swept baskets and papers off his table including a full cup of coffee. Launching into me like a mad man his face turned so red I thought his head would burst. My initial reaction was to be offended that this person who I'd had such a good relationship with had turned against me, so I went into cold statue mode and just stared out of the window at a woman with a pram and dog. He ranted and raved about my report, but it was the word discrimination which really pushed him over the edge. I reminded him of our earlier conversation and how he'd told me that if I wasn't prepared to move it would effect my service. I had this feeling I was actually winning the argument.

'You've a chip on your shoulder the size of Grey's Monument mister.'

'Yes sir … well if I have, somebody must have put it there.'

'Get out you cheeky bastard, I'll have you on point duty the rest of your service. Get out.'

'Am I not allowed to speak sir?'

'What?'

'I used to look up to you sir as a fair man. You always bragged your door was always open and it was, but since you got promoted and moved up here nobody can get to you. Instead of Jack Martin … it's now Chief Superintendent BEM. They've cut your wings, you've sold out.'

'Get out! Get out!' and he rushed round the desk. I was convinced he was going to hit me.

'Going to hit me for telling the truth are you sir?' and stared at him, 'And if you did, do you think I'd let you?'

By now he was apoplectic, 'GET OUT!' I turned to leave.

'Stop!' I turned.

'Yes sir?'

'This doesn't change my original views of you lad.'

'Aye, whatever they were in the first place.'

'Get out!' he screamed again and I left. That's it I thought, I'm finished, but a couple of weeks later I received a hand written note from him which read, 'Report to the Chief's Office Monday morning in your best uniform.' He never said why, but I must have made my point, for come Monday I was promoted uniform section sergeant and posted to the West End Division where a brand new learning curve awaited. I was now a supervisor and very soon realised what everyone had been trying to tell me all those years – how I ever got away with my policing style and attitude, I will never know. Now, having to control men was a different ball game entirely and I was about to begin a further tip toe in a brand new tunic.

THE ROLLERCOASTER CONTINUES

After eleven years as a 'street cop' Arthur McKenzie was promoted Uniform Sergeant to Newcastle West End in 1970 and quickly put in charge of the plain clothes department specialising in Vice Matters. After 18 months his move into CID as a Detective Sergeant was unprecedented being the first officer at that rank, in the force, to be transferred into CID without having served as a Detective Constable.

Four years on he moved into the Drugs Squad and a year later transferred to Newburn Sub Division on promotion to Detective Inspector. In 1977 he was seconded to the No 2 Regional Crime Squad, and later that year was successful in applying for a post in Hong Kong, working for the Independent Commission Against Corruption as a drugs intelligence officer.

On return to Northumbria he served as Uniformed Inspector in Washington and then to Newburn, remaining there until 1985 – in many ways squaring the circle. A posting into Northumbria Crime Intelligence Department took him back into CID as Detective Inspector and in 1987 he returned to the West End in charge of the Sub Divisional CID.

Upon retirement in 1989 he was holding the rank of Acting Divisional Detective Chief Inspector.

His service continued to be a constant source of adventure, wonderment and daily drama and on his last day on duty he literally walked away from Newcastle Crown Court having secured a conviction in a particularly violent murder. A fitting end to a wide and varied career in which he was commended on no less than 27 occasions for exemplary police work.

Hero hauls brothers from quarry

By ARTHUR FAIRLEY

TWO BROTHERS escaped death by inches in a dramatic rescue from a killer quarry.

The boys were only saved through the quick thinking and sheer strength of their rescuers after friends raised the alarm.

It happened when Anthony Turner, 13, and brother Thomas, ten, fell into a claypit in Fatfield, Washington, on Saturday.

Two friends raised the alarm, and Frank Adams, 25, of nearby Victoria Bridge House, came to the rescue.

He said: "I had no idea how badly trapped they were, but decided to take a rope along. If I hadn't they would probably have died.

One stage

"When I got there the young one was up to his waist and going down fast. I used a plank to walk on and pulled him out with the rope, but I couldn't shift his heavier brother."

The prompt arrival of Washington police prevented a tragedy.

Weight-lifting Insp. Arthur McKenzie, 41, helped free Anthony, while Mr Adams kept his head above the slurry.

Mr Adams said : "I was trying to free as much mud around his leg as possible and the inspector managed to pull him out by lifting him under the armpits."

Insp. McKenzie, who is also a discus thrower, said: "There was one stage where although I didn't panic, it became extremely serious. It boiled down to brute strength."

The men were helped by Sgt. Ernie Rowntree and PC David Bonner, who waded waist high in the mud to aid the rescue.

Anthony and Thomas were taken to the Queen Elizabeth Hospital in Gateshead, where they were bathed and warmed up.

Last night Anthony said: "All I could think of was that I was going to die. We will never go back there again."

Supt. David Lander said: "I thought those lads were going to lose their teeth they were shaking that much.

"They were like mummies encased in freezing mud. If Mr Adams hadn't been there they would have been sucked down without trace. We would probably never have discovered them."

Last night Mr Adams, who is unemployed, received high praise from Supt. Lander.

He said: "No words can express the heroism of that man. His determination prevented a tragedy."

Meanwhile, warning notices were being erected yesterday around the old quarry which is to be fenced off.

The rescue of Anthony and Thomas Turner from a claypit in Washington made the local newspapers. Here are the two lads – safe and sound – with myself, Frank Adams (who played a vital role in the rescue), Sergeant Ernie Rowntree and PC David Bonner. A proud moment for all of us.

Not content with a full police career he also drove his energies into sport and whilst he majored in athletics, in his early life he was a Youth International Rugby player, played football at North Shields and represented the National Association of Boys Clubs at Basketball gaining County honours.

He competed at National level in weightlifting from 1966-1970 and was Yorkshire and North East Heavyweight Champion on several occasions and National Police Champion from 1966-1987.

It was as a discus thrower he excelled however, earning vests as International in the British Team from 1962 – 1970, holding the English Native Record for a period and travelling the World on International duty. Highlight of that career was fourth place at the Commonwealth Games in Edinburgh 1970 and his North Eastern Discus Record of 54.25 metres has stood unbroken since 1968 – something of which he is particularly proud.

Dominating National Police Athletics for twenty years he represented them in European Police Championships on no less than five separate occasions, captaining the team in 1982. He also represented his country as a shotputter and from 1979 until the mid nineties was consistently British Veterans Champion in shot, discus and hammer disciplines.

Since retiring as a police officer Arthur has firmly established himself as a writer for stage, radio and television. Since 1980 he has been involved in productions ranging from children's theatre groups and popular television series, working with many companies in developing ideas for programmes.

His first radio play 'The Boilerhunters' – the bawdy tale of a rowdy club bus trip to Blackpool was first transmitted on Radio 4's prestigious Saturday Night Theatre in 1985. Followed up by 'River Rats' his stage play for The People's Theatre which won the Maritime Festival for New Drama in 1986. Other stage shows followed, in particular 'My Son's On The Force' written for the late Sammy Johnson and directed by Tim

Training at the Ouseburn Tip at Byker – 'All hair and ambition'.

My Commonwealth Games passport Edinburgh, 1970. Having won the Commonwealth Trials the Selectors had to pick me for the Games in Edinburgh. There was much aggravation from the other competitors leading up to my event so I left the Commonwealth Village and came home for a couple of days – and enjoyed family life which put it all into perspective. I even found time to see

ORGANISING COMMITTEE'S
OFFICIAL STAMP

1 4 JUL 1970

Date

(Signature of Holder)

ATHLETICS
(Sport)   (Block letters)

COMPETITOR
(Official position)   (Block letters)

For Organising Committee

McKENZIE
(Surname)   (Block letters)

ARTHUR
(Given Name(s))   (Block letters)

THE
BRITISH COMMONWEALTH
GAMES ASSOCIATION

OF   ENGLAND
(Country)

certifies that the holder of this identity card is attending the Games in Edinburgh in the stated capacity.

K.S. Duncan.

Date   Chairman or Secretary

The Scottish Automatic Printing Co., Ltd., Edinburgh. 15

'Born Free' which gave much inspiration. I returned on the day of my event and narrowly missed out on a Bronze medal. True to form my success has YET to be reported in the local papers. But that's throwing events isn't it – described to me one day by Brendan Forster as 'circus events'.

Flag Carrier for the British Police Athletics Team in Zurich, 1982.

As a villain once said to me: 'I know you're a playwright but can you play right?' Two posters for my play, 'My Son's On The Force', a show specially written for actor and close friend Sammy Johnson who went on to public acclaim as the character 'Stick' in the TV series 'Spender'. Gone but certainly not forgotten.

Healy toured the North East in 1987. Since then other actors have performed this piece in Spain, London and it was a part of the Peter Brook Festival at the Gulbenkian Theatre in 1994.

He worked with the Backworth Youth Theatre on a hard hitting piece about glue sniffing in 1980 called 'Sniffer' and in 1988 'Exclusive' – a fantasy dealing with the corruption of young people who aspire to success in sport was specially written for The People's Youth Theatre tour of Russia.

'Man In A Bottle' a joint stage production by Tyne Theatre Company and Live Theatre Newcastle explored the problems of a group of policemen who investigate an indecent assault with tragic consequences. Directed by the late Ken Hill in 1988 this became Arthur's turning point as he moved into television.

Learning his trade on 'The Bill' he wrote twenty four episodes in under fourteen months. Other credits include many television series such as 'Casualty', 'Harry', 'Sam Saturday' and 'Wycliffe' for which he penned several episodes. He wrote many of the dramatic sketches for the award winning 'Voices Of War' a Tyne Tees production for Channel 4 in 1988. In another direction completely he created and produced 'I Married A Great Train Robber' an in depth documentary on Ronnie Biggs and his former wife Charmian for Channel 4's Cutting Edge Programme in 1996. He also co-produced 'Carrickfergus United' for Sky

– a documentary focusing on a group of fanatical Northern Irish Manchester United supporters on their incredible treble success in 1999.

More recently he has completed a screenplay entitled 'The Road' for a Newcastle based film company. Set in the Scottish Isles, this is the story of a crofter who at the age of 66 decides to build a road on a remote island in order to save the community. A stage play 'Standing In The Stalls' the story of a City toilet attendant with ambitions for the stage was performed at the Newcastle Art Theatre in 1999 and was a huge success.

For twenty years he has researched, along with international running coach, Stan Long, the story of James Rowan, the first ever 'Great North Runner' – a World Champion from Gateshead in the late 1800s who flew to the stars and died a pauper. This is still very much in development as a screenplay and stageplay.

Many film companies have sought his services in developing potential ideas and he is at present writing the biography of Steve Black the Newcastle Falcons and British Lions conditioning coach. He is also working closely with former world cruiserweight boxing champion Glenn McCrory on a highly emotive stage play 'Carrying David' which focuses on his brother who had severe muscular dystrophy.

His radio play 'Five Joes And A Gym' – a black comedy which focuses on the lives of five mates who meet in a gym on a daily basis to discus their infirmities was recorded and transmitted in June 2001.

Added to this welter of work, which is in no way definitive, he regularly appears on radio as a pundit and as a member of the National Union of Journalists writes articles for magazines and newspapers. Tyne Tees Television have recently filmed and showed a six-part documentary on his life and times in the 1950s and '60s as a young copper in Newcastle which has served as the basis for this book.

The media may be regarded as a factory where fantasy, creativity and personality thrive. But it's not an industry renowned for terms like loyalty, trust and honesty. Arthur McKenzie is a rare gem who embodies all these attributes. A wonderfully creative writer and one of the most genuine men I have ever met. The key to Arthur is his brilliant sense of humour which pervades everything he does from his superb plays and scripts to his dealings with people.

Arthur cares deeply about the characters he dreams up as well as those real people who surround him. The depth of his caring makes his characters even stronger but also effects all those who meet him. That sense of humanity which drew him into the caring profession of police work has helped shape his writing work and coloured it with that extra layer of sensitivity and feeling.

Arthur is and will remain a proud son of the north and I am proud to be among his friends.

Bob Whittaker
Head of Factual Programmes at London News Network

'It is not a matter of form. This form or that form or of any form whatsoever.'

This conviction of the Russian playwright Anton Chekov taken as his pre-requisite for good drama is aptly borne out in the work of Arthur McKenzie.

A natural storyteller. What he has lived, he has learned. The provenance of his work is in the lives and memories of those he has encountered while on the 'beat', in the city streets or patrolling the docks and quaysides of the small town, which I have the good fortune to share with him as a birthplace.

In every sense a big man. He compels attention, not least for his courage and his honesty. He portrays the incidents of his professional life as fearlessly as he lived them, and with a leavening of good humour that is to his credit and our delight.

Tom Hadaway

The man who changed my life – with Tom Hadaway in 1994. It was Tom who suggested that, 'I should write a play.' When I asked him how I could do that he replied, 'It's your play son – you write it.' The best advice I ever received and I'll always be in Tom's debt for his support and friendship.

Acknowledgements

It is impossible to acknowledge all those deserving of thanks, but I have been blessed with some wonderful friends and inspiration enemies. This tome was started in 1978 and consistently rejected by many publishers, so I take my hat off to Andrew Clark of The People's History for having the bottle to run with it and the patient of Jobe in editing what must have been a nightmare of words. Eric Hollerton of North Shields Library also has my thanks for actually setting the ball rolling for me. Photographs have been used with the permission of Newcastle Library and George Nairn.

I have received much support from many people, but Paul Heslop a friend and colleague of 40 years has been tireless in his efforts and encouragement to see me through this book from start to finish. As for the groups of liars who have said such embarrassing things about me. Why argue? In particular, I would like to thank a small group of highly influential and once powerful men who were directly responsible for their motivational stimulation in giving me a brand new career. They know who they are, but I will be extremely surprised if they are prepared to step out of the shadows and take a bow.

This is not the end.

They say you get more pleasure from your grandchildren.
They are dead right!

Above: After 25 years I still can't get it off the ground even with my grandchildren as well as my children's help. Left to right: Kirsty, Philip, me, Andrew and Samuel.

Left: Marte and Samuel happy in Amsterdam.

Far left: Hekla proudly shows off her medal for gymnastics in Iceland.

Left: Philip at fourteen – carrying on the mantle as a County Discus Champion.

Proud of every one of them – God bless 'em.